/

Moneypower

Also by Ben Stein

ON THE BRINK (with Herbert Stein) 1977
THE CROESUS CONSPIRACY 1978
DREEMZ 1978
THE VIEW FROM SUNSET BOULEVARD 1979

Moneypower

How to Make Inflation Make You Rich

BEN STEIN

with

HERBERT STEIN

HARPER & ROW, PUBLISHERS

NEW YORK

Cambridge
Hagerstown
Philadelphia
San Francisco

1817

London
Mexico City
São Paulo
Sydney

Grateful acknowledgment is made for permission to reprint:

Chart: "The Price of Gold (Gold & Floating Currencies)" by Roy W. Jastram. Reprinted by permission of the *Wall Street Journal.* © 1978 Dow Jones & Company, Inc. All rights reserved.

FIRST EDITION

Designer: Stephanie Winkler

Library of Congress Cataloging in Publication Data

Stein, Benjamin, 1944–
   Moneypower.
      Includes index.
      1. Finance, Personal. 2. Inflation (Finance)
I. Stein, Herbert, joint author. II. Title.
HG179.S83 1979   332'.024   79–2235
ISBN 0–06–014073–9

79 80 81 82 83 10 9 8 7 6 5 4 3 2 1

*For Rachel Epstein, for Larry Lissitzyn and
for Linda Fairstein*

Contents

PART THREE
Behavior Modification: The Inflation School
and Its Lessons

Preface

I decided to write this book for several reasons. First, about three years ago my father and I wrote a novel—*On the Brink*—about a hypothetical hyperinflation and what it would do to daily life in America. In that book we were talking about far faster inflation than we are likely to face any time soon. But in researching that book, we discovered certain facts about inflations of the past.

One discovery was that certain behavior in investing and selling and borrowing almost always made people rich in inflationary periods. Over long periods, the same forces were at work. It seemed to me to be a secret that more people should be let in on. Hence this *Moneypower* book, which lets the reader know just how it was done.

The second motivation was seeing lots of friends making money during an inflationary period at a terrific clip while others, just as worthy in every meaningful sense, were left high and dry, punished every day by inflation. There was no flaw in the losers' makeup as compared with the winners'. The losers simply did not know the rules and the winners did.

Once again, it occurred to me that it was a good idea to share the secret. The number of people who can profit from inflation should not be limited to those with family in the real estate business or the gold business and so forth.

And as a further motivation, I realized that there was simply a great deal of ignorance out there about how the rules of prudent money management change during an inflation. And since I had studied the subject in books and in real life, I thought I could write a book that would shed some light on the subject.

In writing this book, I had enormous help, most of it from my family. My father contributed greatly to the portions of the book about the genesis of inflation and the warning signals as to when it is likely to end, if ever. In addition, he carefully read the manuscript and corrected me where enthusiasm exceeded prudence. The book could not possibly have been written without his careful advice, given over the years, about what to do in a period of steadily rising prices. (All specific investment advice is mine alone.)

My wonderful wife spent long hours in libraries and brokerage offices tracking the records of various investments, finding out the best ways to borrow, and basically doing the most detailed research. She encouraged me when I became tired.

My mother read the manuscript with an eagle eye and corrected whatever faulty grammar or stylistic construction there was. If the book flows smoothly, it is largely thanks to her.

And my sister contributed large numbers of useful real-life anecdotes about the sorrow of not understanding the MONEY-POWER rules of inflation, and the joys of getting on the inflation bandwagon with the help of a little knowledge.

Outside my family, I am deeply indebted to Jim Bellows, who first realized how eager people were to learn about how to use inflation to make money; to Allen Priaulx, who helped get the concept before the nation as a syndicated series; to Walter Meade of Avon Books, who encouraged me to write the program in book form; and to Erwin Glikes and Barbara Grossman, of Harper & Row, who were likewise enthusiastic.

All of us stand in debt to Professor Milton Friedman, who, along with Anna Schwartz, first explained the genesis of inflation in a convincing way and repeatedly taught us, through writings and in person, how the system is stacked in favor of borrowers and against lenders. I am likewise grateful to Professor Lowell Harriss, who explained to me just how the economy worked in terms that even I could understand as a college student, and to Michael Greene, who taught me about exotic cars.

And also I thank Peter M. Flanigan, who inspired me with the basic idea that in this world there is nothing stopping us from getting the things we want out of life except our own inertia. "Go do it," Peter Flanigan said to me many years ago, and I have not stopped since. Nor should the reader of this book.

The reader should read the following: No economic conditions last forever. We are presently in the midst of a severe inflation. Those who follow the *Moneypower* rules during this period will be grateful. But nothing lasts forever. At some point far down the road there may be a ghastly recession and inflation may recede. It can happen. For now, *Moneypower* sums up the way we live today. It may not last forever. You will be able to read about it in the papers when inflation comes to an end. Then file away *Moneypower* for the next inflation.

But for today, prices are rising at an all-time peacetime rate. Tens of millions of people are in financial quicksand. *Moneypower* will let you build real castles, not sand, while others about you are washed away. It is the way to make inflation make you rich.

Moneypower

Introduction:
Getting to Know
the Real World

The only way to beat inflation is to have more money. Getting that money by making inflation work for you is what MONEYPOWER is all about.

In the eleven years between 1967 and 1979 the consumer price index rose by over 106 percent.

The real income of American families, adjusted for inflation and for taxes, usually just barely kept pace. The real earnings of American families on the average fell well behind the costs of:

- Health care, including hospital stays
- Homeownership
- Maintenance of an automobile
- Food consumed at home, including, meat, poultry, fish, fruits, and vegetables
- Food consumed in restaurants
- Utilities of all kinds

In today's era of hyperinflation, no one can count on wages to automatically keep raising our standard of living. The grim fact is that for the last decade and longer, for a variety of reasons, almost a majority of American families have seen their standard of living stagnate and erode as wages continue to fail to keep ahead of inflation. We have entered a long-term phase in which the breadwinner who counts on the general tide of prosperity to keep him ahead of inflation is counting on a phantom.

Inflation, combined with low productivity, changing population patterns, and lack of discipline in the workplace, has led to a flattening of real wages after taxes and inflation over the last decade. Inflation alone has left tens of millions of families' incomes lower in terms of what they will actually buy than they were ten years ago. On the average, almost half of the families in the United States have failed to keep pace with inflation in terms of their incomes. Their standard of living has actually fallen.

As if that were not bad enough, the net worth of millions of American families has been hacked away by inflation until the families stand financially naked before the storms of life. Every family that trusted to keeping all its money in the bank has lost out—is actually poorer now than it was ten years ago. The families that kept their precious nest eggs in stocks or bonds are generally poorer right now than they were ten years ago. No one can count on his savings staying worth what they were worth the day they became savings.

Nor can a wage earner count on his sweat keeping his standard of living up to the level of a decade ago. For many workers, their standard of living simply falls farther and farther behind. If the family needs unusually large amounts of food or fuel or medical care, it falls even farther behind.

For the man or woman who is determined to beat inflation, who is determined to improve his or her family's life in the face of inflation, there is only one solution: Direct, individual action to make more money.

And for the individual who wants to make money in an era of continuous inflation, there is only one best way to do so: He must harness the immense forces of inflation in order to create wealth.

MONEYPOWER is the science of how to use your money

and your labor in such a way that the same forces that drive up prices drive up your earnings and your assets far faster than inflation in the economy. MONEYPOWER is a map that can guide you to a plateau of financial security far higher than the waves of inflation can reach, using as motive power the forces of inflation.

MONEYPOWER is neither exclusively for the seasoned investor nor solely for the neophyte wage earner. MONEYPOWER is for anyone who can add and subtract and can see what is going on around him. MONEYPOWER is the application of the laws of economics, specifically the laws of economics in the age of inflation, to real life on the ground.

MONEYPOWER tells how the individual investor and worker can take a small amount of money and by placing it judiciously make inflation turn it into a large amount of money. MONEYPOWER tells how properly invested small sums can grow far faster than the rate of inflation by capturing the strength of inflation and taming it to your own advantage.

MONEYPOWER applies strictly to the age of inflation. It reveals what cunning speculators have known since before the Christian era about how inflation greatly raises the value of some assets—far more than the rate of inflation itself. MONEYPOWER explains how certain types of purchasing—primarily purchasing with borrowed money—harnesses vast energy to vault high above the general rise in prices.

MONEYPOWER is not about finding bargains in the age of inflation. It is not about lowering your living standard to cope with inflation.

MONEYPOWER has nothing whatsoever to do with plans for lessening the scale of a family's defeat from inflation.

MONEYPOWER has everything to do with triumphing in the age of inflation, because of inflation, using inflation to make yourself rich in many cases.

MONEYPOWER extends the subject of how inflation can be made to work for you to successful buying, working, and retirement in the age of inflation. In every area, MONEYPOWER calls for understanding the forces of inflation—and making them work for you. MONEYPOWER is not hiding in the storm cellar while the inflationary storm rages. This particular storm may take another ten years to subside. MONEYPOWER is about grasping the electricity of the storm and harnessing it to light the way to prosperity beyond what most persons would think possible.

MONEYPOWER is a strategy of individual effort, guided by systematically gathered knowledge about how inflation affects various prices. It calls for study, concentration, effort, and risk by each and every person who is determined to win big in the age of inflation. MONEYPOWER has nothing to do with consumer boycotts or political campaigns. It has nothing to say about which candidate to vote for in an election. It has everything to say about voting for yourself to make some real money.

Before we race forward into the heart of MONEYPOWER— how to make and save and earn money in the age of inflation— the MONEYPOWER investor should know a few preliminaries.

First, in order to beat inflation it is important to know where inflation comes from. In a word, it comes from the federal government and from nowhere else. Here's how it happens:

Imagine that inflation is a balloon. Its surface is many prices that are enlarged and expanded as the inflation increases and the balloon becomes more monstrous. Everyone knows that the balloon cannot blow itself up. By the same token, in the real-life economy, prices cannot raise themselves. One or more factors in the economy may try to raise prices, but a general price rise cannot stick because there is simply no way for the economy to pay out the money to keep the prices up, unless someone blows hot air into the balloon. Or unless someone blows money into the economy to keep the prices up, just as the hot air keeps the balloon up.

The money supply of the country determines the level of

prices in the country, just as the amount of air in a balloon determines the girth of a balloon. The supply of money in the United States is controlled entirely by the federal government, through the Federal Reserve Board, and more particularly through the operations of the Federal Open Market Committee. That means just what it seems like it means: the federal government determines the level of inflation by the amount of money it creates.

While there is some dispute about the amount of time that is required for the changes in the money supply of the United States to be reflected in inflation, it is clear that with a lag, which may be about two years, the operations of the Federal Open Market Committee can be seen at the grocery and department store.

To adopt another analogy, imagine that the federal government flies over a small, isolated town, dropping stacks of twenty-dollar bills out the hatch of the plane. Naturally, everyone in the town will have lots of money. Naturally, prices will go up, as the flush townspeople bid up everything with their newfound wealth. This, on a larger scale, is just what has happened to the United States in recent years. The money has rolled out of the Federal Reserve Board, and the prices have skyrocketed.

Labor unions cannot raise prices because there can be no price rise without a rise in the supply of money any more than a tire can be inflated without more air being pumped into it. Rapacious businessmen or crafty foreigners cannot raise prices either—unless there is a rise in the stock of money. Individual prices of separate goods and services can rise, but there can be no rise that persists through the economy in general without an increase in the money supply.

To understand why the United States has had such serious inflation for the last decade and for long before, one need only know that the stock of money in the economy has almost tripled since 1968.

And if all of this could be simplified into one phrase, it

would be this: Inflation is too much money chasing too few goods. And the government has made sure that there will be too much money in the system for almost any quantity of goods. The entire country has been flooded with money just as the small town in our example has been bombarded with money from an airplane.

The government creates all this money by a simple expedient. The Federal Reserve System is the only lawful money-creating agency in this country. It works by writing checks upon itself. These checks are then the lawful money of the land. There need be no backing, either of gold or of anything else, for the money the Federal Reserve creates.

When the federal government needs to cover its deficit, the Federal Reserve creates money to ease the plight of the lenders—or simply lends the money itself. When the economy appears to be slowing down, the Federal Reserve pumps money into the system to speed it up by making loans easier to get. For almost any occasion, the Federal Reserve stands ready to create money—and does so.

Thus, the Federal Reserve and the federal officials who influence it create the inflation. They do so because they believe that creating money is the surest way to keep the economy from backsliding into recession or depression. Rarely in the postwar period has the Federal Reserve shown any inclination to genuinely crack down on the creation of money so as to wring all inflation out of the economy. There is scant evidence that in the future this policy will change.

Therefore, when politicians and their creatures have their hands on the levers of power, few people can expect that they will risk high unemployment and recession by slowing down the growth of the money stock. Hence, more money and ever higher prices in the past and into the future.

Inflation is not going away until politicians change their spots.

Second, those people who have believed the federal government when the federal government said that it would stop inflation have been doomed to severe, punishing disappointment. One of the stock promises of politicians is to guarantee that there will be an end to inflation during their Administration. One of the stock facts of life is that it never happens. Since the Administration of Harry S Truman, Presidents have been promising that there will be no more inflation. Seven Presidents later, we have the worst two-year period of inflation in peacetime history.

Those who believe the promises of the politicians that things will get better deserve what they get in the way of financial comeuppance. It is always possible that someday an honest politician will appear to save us from the inflationary monster. But it is about as likely as the appearance of creatures from outer space in your backyard. Someday it will surely happen, but it is somewhat wasteful to wait for it.

Third, when Scarlett O'Hara visited Rhett Butler in a Union jail after the end of the Civil War, he told her he was rich. She was amazed, because everyone she knew, in the aftermath of the tragic war, was poor.

"There is just as much money to be made from the tearing down of a civilization as from the building up of a civilization," Rhett said. And he was right.

An investor who understands the dynamics of inflation knows that there is just as much money to be made during the era of hyperinflation as in periods of price stability. In fact, in some ways it is easier to make real money during a period of hyperinflation than during any other time.

In all the major recorded eras of hyperinflation, speculators who followed the easily observed rules of price behavior have been able to quite predictably make money on sweeping price changes that moved in advance of the general trends of inflation.

During the American Civil War, enormous, staggering profits were made by speculators who predicted—and with perfect reason—that the price of gold would move far in advance of the price of other commodities. The same was true during the hyperinflation that followed World War I.

During the great Weimar inflation that culminated in 1923, alert German speculators turned all of their assets into dollars. They found themselves richer than their wildest imaginings because of the incredible run-up in the value of the dollar as compared with the mark. As the rest of their countrymen floundered around in the morass of inflation, alert Germans harnessed the overwhelming force of inflation to make incalculable fortunes.

Today in America the same possibilities exist. Today's inflation is fully as rich in possibilities for wealth and fortune as the inflations of times past.

Inflation is simply a new set of circumstances that demand adjustment, just like prosperity or depression. Once the wide-awake citizen realizes that he is in a totally new ball game with totally new rules, he can start playing to win. There are just as many runs to be made in night games as in day games.

And that is yet another point of MONEYPOWER strategy. There is a whole new set of rules for playing in this inflationary world, and he who keeps trying to play by the same old rules is bound to be disappointed indeed. Imagine trying to play water polo by the rules of tennis, and you have some idea of just how futile it is to attempt to make money during a period of price inflation using the rules of price stability.

For a key example, consider the common advice that borrowing or lending is a mistake. Not true. Although a loan might have often lost both itself and friend in Elizabethan days, the same loan might make a person well-heeled during a depression. And although borrowing might dull the edge of husbandry during price stability, it is the only way to make money during the era of hyperinflation.

The old rules lead to nothing but frustration and disappointment in today's world. Put them away in the back of your mind for a future day—long in the future perhaps—of price stability. For the present, for real time, as the computer experts say, learn the new rules of MONEYPOWER. Again, they will not apply forever. Someday *everyone* in the country will catch on to the need to expect continuous inflation, and bargains in various investments will disappear. But that day is far off. Someday inflation will slow, and investors will no longer be able to expect spectacular year-to-year gains in various fields. But that day is a long way off. For now, MONEYPOWER is the rule of the day. Someday soon, we may go into a recession. If it is slight, the inflation will hardly be slowed at all. If it is severe, it will be a prelude to yet another burst of inflation. In either case MONEYPOWER will apply.

Equally important to knowing the new rules of the game is bearing in mind the basic simplicity of the MONEYPOWER strategy. It does not involve complex manipulations of price/earnings ratios or of bond yields. It involves the basic concept of buying low and selling high. MONEYPOWER lays out quite clearly that the key way of "buying low" in the inflationary era is to buy with borrowed money. For if the entire essence of what man has learned about how to behave during an inflation were to be summed up in one word, that word would be *borrow*.

And if the entire corpus of knowledge about how to make money on a big scale during inflation were to be summed up in a single sentence, that sentence would be: *Borrow to make money on certain goods and properties that rise in value faster than inflation.*

And the final point of the MONEYPOWER strategy is the simplest of all. *You* can make money during an inflationary era—substantial money—but you must do it yourself. There is no substitute for victory in war. In making money during the era of inflation there is no substitute for action taken by the investor, purchaser, wage earner. No sensible person can count on anyone else to do it for him or her. No government will do it. Similarly, no boss or union can or will do it.

MONEYPOWER is a strategy of personal commitment to action to defeat inflation. Real-world actions, not broodings or pious hopes, will defeat inflation.

If you want to make money—real money—from inflation, you will succeed with MONEYPOWER if you count on yourself to help yourself.

Let us now make some real money.

PART ONE

A House Is More Than a Home

1

The Single-Family Home:
A Heavenly Hedge

The best way to learn about the actual day-to-day workings of the MONEYPOWER strategy is to follow an example of what makes a good MONEYPOWER investment. By studying what goes into the best of inflation-beating vehicles, we can see what the basic qualities of a successful MONEYPOWER investment are. There is a saying in law schools that the most valuable course is the one that teaches you how to find the courthouse. By the same token, the most valuable MONEYPOWER method of teaching is to show the investor just where the money tree grows.

In this case, it grows in the backyard of that great American dream—the privately owned home.

The ideal MONEYPOWER hedge against inflation would:

- Rise in value faster—even far faster—than the rate of inflation
- Be highly leveraged, so that you mostly used other people's money to make your money—this is a must
- Yield enormous tax benefits in every phase of its acquisition, maintenance, and sale
- Carry with it government subsidies for most facets of its existence
- Serve a crucial function, offering an irreplaceable service while it makes money for you
- Be bought and sold in a highly liquid market, so that sales and

purchases can be consummated quickly, without undue friction in terms of either time or money.

• Be immune to daily or weekly or monthly large-scale fluctuations in its price
• Offer the promise of continued high rises in value far into the future
• Allow the buyer to pay with borrowed valuable dollars and repay with worthless dollars

This is an imperfect world, and there is no such investment, but there is one that satisfies almost every requirement. The good old privately owned home, whether it is a free-standing house, a duplex, or a condominium, meets every test except that of liquidity.

Before we go through them, point by point, and match the ideal with the real in terms of housing, historical examples might be of great value.

From the days of the decline and fall of the Roman Empire (to coin a phrase), people have known, and historians have recorded, the virtual immunity of real estate to inflations. Edward Gibbon, in his *Decline and Fall of the Roman Empire,* points out that as the emperors debased the coinage to pay for their vainglory and their wars, landowners demanded—and got—even greater numbers of the smaller gold pieces, so that the actual *weight* of gold that they got for their land did not vary.

In other words, even in the days of barbarians at the gates, when every other commodity was phenomenally costly and ordinary citizens were literally going hungry because they could not pay the inflated prices, owners of land stayed prosperous because of the rapidly rising value of their land. Real estate in the days of the Caesars consistently kept its owners insulated from the hazards of inflation, if we are to believe Gibbon.

In the worst days of the thirteenth century, according to Barbara Tuchman, inflation was rampant. Kings and princes regularly inflated their coinage to pay an ever-growing mountain of debt from war and pageantry. And, as the value of the money declined, the owners of land commanded ever greater rents, so that they, too, like their counterparts in Roman days, kept well above the battle in terms of inflation.

What landowners did twenty centuries ago and seven centuries ago is exactly what we want to do today. While our currency is collapsing in value we want to own something that rises in value faster than money declines, so that we are actually making money on inflation.

For that wonderful goal, a private home is made to order.

First, a brief and painless excursion into the theory of just why private homes are such a fine inflation hedge. It will be a short trip.

Inflation is first and foremost, to repeat, too much money chasing too few goods. The best kinds of goods to have, therefore, are goods that take a long time to create, so that you can be sure there will always be too few of them. That means a house. With ever-increasing mountains of red tape and bureaucratic time-wasting standing between the idea of building a home and the reality of a finished home, it now takes more than two years for the average home to get built. Materials shortages, ranging from lumber to cement to insulation, slow down the process further. Compliance with old and, even worse, new building codes takes still more time. And anyone who has ever had a contractor work on anything knows that getting five consecutive days of work out of a contractor takes a good six months.

So houses will continue to be, for the foreseeable future, on the "too few" end of the equation of too much money chasing too few goods.

Further, because houses are almost always bought with borrowed money—mortgages—the home buyer gets in on the other end of the equation as well. Whenever the government wants to pump up the economy—which is almost all the time—

remember, the prime method it uses is to create more money. That money floods the banks and they have great chunks of money to lend for home mortgages—at rates that are phenomenally low. (That may sound incredible in the days of 11 percent mortgages, but just hold your breath. In the age of 10 percent inflation, an 11 percent mortgage is almost free.)

So the banks stuff money into the prospective home buyers' pockets with both hands, and the would-be homeowners wildly (after a fashion) bid against each other for the available houses.

And so the homeowner is sitting in the catbird seat. He takes advantage of the "too much money" part as well as the "too few goods" part of the equation that causes inflation.

Now why is a house so good at beating inflation? Let us take it point by point.

The ideal inflation hedge would rise in value faster—even far faster—than the rate of inflation.

Since 1942, the average of all consumer prices has risen by over 300 percent. The market basket of all the things the average family buys costs four times as much as at the time of Wake Island. But the value of the average single-family house has risen by over 600 percent since 1945.

Take a more recent time period, and you get an even more dramatic picture. Since 1967, the Consumer Price Index has risen by more than 100 percent—as of this writing. In other words, prices have more than doubled in the last eleven years.

But the average single-family home has risen in value by almost 200 percent—twice as fast as the general level of inflation. Taking an even more recent period, since 1973, whereas the Consumer Price Index has risen at an average rate of about 7.5 percent, housing prices have risen by an average rate of about 11 percent.

These are numbers from government agencies and from trade associations. They include houses in Newark and the South Bronx, as well as houses in Beverly Hills and River Oaks. Anyone knows that prices in good neighborhoods have consistently risen far faster than the 11 percent the government describes as a national average. In fact, in the good neighborhoods of our large cities, price rises of 2 to 3 percent per *month* have not been unusual in recent years.

Leaving theories behind, why has housing gone up in price so incredibly quickly? The main reason that any commodity rises in value far above the cost of producing it is that people believe it will cost far more in the future. And, quite simply and quite soundly, Americans believe that houses will be even more expensive in the future than they are now.

Steadily, remorselessly, the prices of everything going into a home have risen. The cost of labor and materials has consistently defied our worst expectations. Who would have believed, even a few years ago, that ordinary laborers, completely untrained, would command more than $50 a day? Who would have believed that ⅜-inch plywood sheets would sell for $15 for a 25-square-foot sheet, or that drywall would go for 50 cents a square foot?

But even more than labor and materials, the price of land in prime locations has skyrocketed. The land component of housing costs has shot up far faster than any other component. There is simply less land left near cities that is esthetically and environmentally useful for building houses. In addition, government restrictions on development have placed a premium on land that can be used for building. So land skyrockets beyond what we would have believed possible only a short time ago.

When people expect that the price of a house will shoot up faster than other prices, and accordingly bid up prices of houses, they have every reason to think that they are right. And, therefore, the prices of houses continue to rise far faster than the rise of other prices generally, and there is no reason to think the prices will stop rising.

(Home prices will surely fluctuate in that some years they will rise more than other years. But the general trend is clearly up, and up faster than the Consumer Price Index.)

Another of the criteria for the ideal inflation hedge is simply that we can confidently expect the price of the hedge to exceed inflation for a long time to come. And that criterion is met not only because of expectations, but because of an interesting and rewarding demographic phenomenon.

It is a statistically verified fact that the age at which new families begin to shop for single-family houses is when the parents reach the ages of thirty to thirty-five. By simple arithmetic, we can figure that the young men and women who are, let us say, thirty-five now were born in 1944, and the young men and women who are thirty now were born in 1949. We also know that the years from 1942 to about 1958 were fantastically fruitful years for the American family. Children were born in large numbers, creating an enormous demand for schools, teachers, teen-age idols, and now—houses.

The wartime and postwar baby booms produced a bumper crop of potential home buyers, who are now actual home buyers. They demand housing far faster than it can be supplied. Moreover, since the postwar baby boom continued well into the 1950s, we can expect a bulge of demand for housing that will continue—at least—well into the 1980s.

Like everything that is in high demand, like everything that is in severely short supply, housing has risen sharply in price. It will continue that way for the foreseeable future.

The second qualification for the ideal MONEYPOWER hedge is that the investment can be leveraged in its purchase, or bought with borrowed money. The private residence satisfies that criterion to a T.

Now, just why is it so important to buy a home or any inflation hedge with borrowed money? The answer is that no ordinary person can make money with just his savings out of his earnings. The hopes of millions of moms and dads to the contrary, notwithstanding, you simply cannot get any real money by saving a few dollars regularly out of your salary. Millions of people have been brainwashed into thinking that if they are sufficiently frugal and sock money away in their savings account instead of spending it on taxicabs or a new pair of shoes, they will eventually acquire wealth.

It never happens. A simple bit of mathematics might explain the problem. If you, the very solid citizen, earn $50,000 a year and, by miracles, nay, prodigies of frugality, can save $5,000 of it, and if you put it in the bank at interest of 6 percent a year, at the end of thirty years you will have very roughly $500,000. But, life does not work out that way. First, you will have to pay about half of your interest earnings in tax. Then, at a 10 percent rate of inflation, you will actually be throwing out $200 of every $5,000 you save—just in the first year. If that inflation rate continues, your $500,000 (or perhaps $400,000 after tax) will actually be worth the equivalent of about $20,000 today—hardly great wealth by anyone's standards. (The interest rate would be slightly higher, but the point is the same.)

No one, absolutely no one, can get rich by saving his own money. All people who get rich do it either by luck or by the judicious use of other people's money.

Or take another example, spiced with a few numbers. If you, again, a solid citizen, borrow $100,000 at 12 percent interest, and use it to buy a valuable widget, which goes up 15 percent per year, you will make $3,000 beyond your interest payments in the first year. If you borrow that money and keep making 3 percent above your costs, you will have a nice present each year. Nothing fancy, but it did not cost you a dime.

But if we take a broader view of life's possibilities, we get a far more rosy picture. If you borrow that same $100,000 at 12 percent and buy something that rises at a 15 percent compounded rate, you are starting to make real money. Your investment will be worth one million dollars in sixteen years.

Your net profit even after interest payments will be about
$300,000.

That is how people become millionaires. Take a more con-
crete example. Say you buy a valuable widget for $100,000
and pay $20,000 down and borrow the rest at 10 percent. If
the widget rises in value by 15 percent per year, at the end
of about five years it is worth $200,000. You still owe $80,000,
so you have made $100,000. (Always, not counting the service
of the loan.) On your initial $20,000, you have made 500 per-
cent profit. This is called leverage. It is the home buyer's best
friend.

Now, all over the world, the usual method of buying a house
is to pay cash or to borrow about half and pay it back in a
short time—say, five years. But in America, we have an entirely
more congenial form of home finance. During the 1930s, some
genius invented the long-term, no-balloon-payment mortgage
with a low down payment. This wonderful idea, confined
largely to the United States, has made homeownership possible
for almost anyone. And almost anyone can use the method
of long-term mortgages to beat inflation.

A private residence in a good location is that very widget
we are looking for. You can buy it with borrowed money
and watch its value skyrocket. You can make far more money
with it than you can by simply saving your pennies. And,
you can make far more money with it than you will have to
pay in interest on your loan.

Just to make sure the point about the critical nature of
leverage gets made, look at it two ways.

First, if homes are doubling in value every four and a half
years—as they are now—and if you pay for your home with
80 percent borrowed money, you will quintuple your money
in four and a half years, discounting your monthly mortgage
payments—which you *should* discount. If you paid all cash
for that home, you would only have doubled your money.
Remember, you only paid 20 percent of the original price,

but you get all the gain. The key is that you are making money with other people's money. Not only are you making money on your down payment—you are also making money on somebody else's money that the bank has lent you.

You are making a few percent on the 20 percent you put down on the house, and you are making a few percent on the 80 percent, too. It all adds up to real money, very quickly.

John D. Rockefeller used to go to sleep each night worried about how he could possibly repay all his borrowings. Each morning he would arise and think of new ways to borrow still more.

The third requisite of an ideal inflation hedge is that it yield enormous tax advantages in its acquisition and sale. Federal and state income taxes take such an enormous bite out of the American family's pocket that careful tax planning is crucial even for a wage earner. For the more highly paid citizen, tax planning is as important as earning.

There is no tax shelter as safe, secure, and rich in possibilities as a private house. Over the years, Presidents and Congresses have heaped upon the homeowner a plethora of tax benefits. They are made to be enjoyed and taken advantage of.

The main tax benefit is that all interest payments are deductible from your income for purposes of computing federal income tax. That is so staggeringly important that its significance takes a while to sink in. When you buy a home with an 80 percent mortgage—the typical method—for the first several years of the duration of the mortgage, almost all of your monthly payment is interest.

For example, if you buy a $60,000 home with $12,000 down, you will have a $48,000 mortgage. Assume that it is a standard thirty-year, 10 percent mortgage. Each month's payment is $421. Of that, $400 is interest and fully tax deductible.

If you are a family with an adjusted gross income of about $25,000, with normal deductions, your marginal rate of tax is about 30 percent.

This means that you save 30 percent of what you pay to the mortgage holder because of your lower income tax. In turn, that means your monthly payments are really less than $305—in real, after-tax dollars.

And, far more important from our point of view, that also means that the effective rate of interest on your mortgage is not 10 percent but 7 percent. In terms of fighting inflation, that makes a major difference.

The gain that you make in fighting inflation can only be measured by taking the increase in value of the property—in this case, a private residence—and deducting from it the cost of acquiring and maintaining the property. The deductibility feature of the interest on mortgages greatly lowers the cost of both acquisition and maintenance of a home.

Look at it with numbers to get the full impact of the tax advantage.

Suppose you buy a piece of property that goes up in value 12 percent in the first year. If you were paying 10 percent on the mortgage, you will be making the full 12 percent on the amount you paid down, and 2 percent (12 minus 10) on the amount you borrowed. (All this is in round numbers. The actual computations are greatly more complex and only slightly different in result.)

But if you take into account the tax-deductibility feature, you will find yourself doing far better. You will make the same 12 percent on your down payment, but you will make 5 percent (12 minus 7) instead of 2 percent on the amount you borrowed (80 percent of the total).

In other words, you will be making a great deal of money on the money you borrowed. In more detail, dollar by dollar, it runs like this. Suppose you buy a house that costs $60,000, and you put down 20 percent, or $12,000, with a $48,000 thirty-year mortgage at 10 percent. The first year, let us assume, the price of the house goes up 12 percent. It increases in value by $7,200, to a total value of $67,200.

In the first year, you will pay $5,052 in mortgage payments. That leaves only a slight gain of about $2,148. But if you take into account the tax-deductibility feature as it applies to mortgage payments, you get a very different picture. Your increase in value is the same, but your costs are very different— each payment really costs you only $280. So, counting $20 a month for reduction of principal, you have monthly payments of $300, or $3,600 a year. Instead of $2,148, you have made $3,600 ($7,200 less $3,600).

And it gets better than that. You made that $3,600 on an initial investment of $12,000, so that in the very first year of homeownership you made about 30 percent profit, which even in 1979 will keep you ahead of inflation.

If the deductibility feature of interest payments was the only good feature of buying a house—tax wise—the homeowner would have gotten a good deal. He would, for the first few years of owning his home, pay only about the nominal mortgage payment times (1 minus his marginal rate of tax). But the deal is not just a good deal, as the used-car dealers say. It is a great deal.

The Congress of the United States, assembled in its majesty, has given special tax benefits to owners of homes when they decide the time is ripe to sell. By taxing the gains on the sale of a house at capital-gains rates or below, the Congress has made homeownership a pleasure going out as well as coming in.

Under the statutes of the United States, a residence is considered a capital asset. That means it qualifies for specially low tax rates on any increase in value. As with all capital assets, held for over one year, 60 percent of the gain is excluded before the tax is applied to that which is not excluded. Thus, with a top rate of 70 percent, the absolute maximum of tax, even on a million-dollar gain, would be 28 percent (70 times .40).

If you had a million dollars of income from bonds, you

would pay $700,000 tax. But if you make a million-dollar gain on real estate, you are going to be taxed only $280,000 at most. And the differences are quite significant even at lower levels.

It is basic to the fight against inflation—your own personal MONEYPOWER crusade—that you take advantage of all the tax laws that leave you with more money than you would otherwise have. And the capital-gains exclusion is just the beginning of the good things that the tax code has in mind for the homeowner.

For most citizens, there simply never is any tax on the capital gains from the sale of a house at all. Never. A marvelous provision of the Internal Revenue Code says that if you use the proceeds of the sale of your principal residence to buy another principal residence of equal or greater value, you can completely forget about the tax. And if the house passes into your estate, your heirs take its value at the time of passing as its basis.

So, for almost everyone, there never is any capital-gains tax on the sale of a private residence. Note well that this escape provision applies to primary residences only and not to second homes or investment property. However, the lower capital-gains rate still does apply to sales of all real estate, no matter what its use.

It is important to keep in mind that a house or other piece of property counts as capital-gains property *only* if it is held for a minimum of one year.

There are goodies in the Internal Revenue Code for all the happy homeowners. Under the 1978 revisions of the Code, very major relief for homeowners over fifty-five was created. It allows a great deal of the gain—sometimes all of it—on the sale of a primary residence to escape taxation, whether or not the proceeds are used to buy another residence.

These new provisions are one-shot deals. They can be invoked only once during transit through this vale of tears. Still, for older people who want to take the money they have in their homes and use it to live on, the new provisions are a godsend. They allow much of inflation-generated gains to completely escape taxation and become available for use simply to live out the remaining span of years allotted to each of us.

In fact, the new provisions are an explicit recognition that the older person's main asset and bulwark against inflation is his house. Of course, a house is almost everyone's main bulwark against inflation—or should be. Check with your lawyer or accountant on the specifics.

Then there are property taxes. State and local governments levy taxes to pay for schools, fire services, hospitals, and so forth. Those taxes are assessed on the value of your home. Those taxes are too high, as people have been discovering lately, but they do have one redeeming feature. They, like interest payments, are fully deductible against income for computing federal income tax.

The beauty of this can best be seen if one compares the homeowner's situation with the renter's situation. The renter pays the landlord for all of the landlord's expenses, including property taxes. That means the renter pays for the property taxes as a portion of his rent. But, of course, the renter cannot deduct a penny of his rental payments, even though a large part of his rent pays the tax-deductible expenses of the landlord.

If you are a homeowner, you can deduct every penny of your payments for state taxes. (To be fair, some might say that in an ideal world the landlord lowers the tenant's rent by however much he saves because of tax deductions. But most landlords live in a world that is far from the ideal.)

Add them up: The three big tax breaks that come with using homeownership as a hedge against inflation are

• Full deductibility of the interest component of mortgage payments

- Vastly preferential treatment of capital gains made on the sale of housing
- Full deductibility of property taxes

The sum total of all of these advantages is that they greatly lower the homeowner's cost of buying, maintaining, and selling a home. That means they generate hugely greater gains as the homeowner watches the value of his house skyrocket.

There is a lot of mathematics associated with the various tax features that benefit a homeowner. But the reader whose eyes glaze over when he is confronted with mathematics or arithmetic can look at it this simple way:

The goal of MONEYPOWER is to own things that will rise in value far faster than the cost of carrying them plus inflation. The many tax advantages described above generate a far lower cost basis and thus put some weight into the old saw of Buy Low—Sell High. They help the homeowner to Buy Low, and thus make more money when he Sells High.

(Inflation, as everyone knows, strikes hardest at the retired citizen, often living on a fixed income. For that special class of citizen, there is yet another tax benefit. Many states and many countries within states allow a preferentially lower rate of property tax for homeowners above a certain age. The age varies from locale to locale, as does the preferentially lower rate. But in some areas of the country, the savings on property taxes for older Americans is more than 50 percent. For the specifics of this tax break in your area, you should visit an accountant or the appropriate local government office.)

The gigantic tax advantages that accrue to homeowners stack the deck in the homeowner's favor as far as getting an investment that will outperform inflation.

So far, what you have when you buy a home as an inflation hedge is an investment that

- Will rise faster than inflation
- Will allow you to make money with other people's money

• Will get you substantial tax savings so as to lower the cost to you of the home

As good as all of that is, there are still other valuable aspects to owning a home. The ideal inflation hedge would serve a crucial and irreplaceable function. What could possibly do that better than a home? The old chestnut that a man's home is his castle has some truth in it. There is a sense of security connected with owning a home, which no other kind of living arrangement can offer.

No landlord can evict you capriciously or raise your rent or make you get rid of your pets. No neurotic janitor can torment you. No vicious building superintendent can refuse to fix your leaky faucet.

These are not specifically inflation-fighting features, but they make life a lot more pleasant when you are in the battle. A home is your best friend in the struggle to keep abreast of inflation, and the best part is in the next chapter.

2

Houses II: Almost Something for Nothing

In the preceding chapter, we began to see why a house, which rises rapidly in value, can be bought with leverage, and which comes with enormous tax advantages, is the ideal vehicle for fighting inflation. All of those things are important and even critical. But the largest advantage in buying a house as the keystone of the MONEYPOWER strategy is that you buy it along a time frame that gives you the absolutely greatest advantage in terms of making inflation and debasement of the currency work for you.

You buy a house with borrowed valuable dollars today and repay with plentiful inflated dollars tomorrow. And that is true bonanza country.

At the beginning of this book we pointed out that inflation offered an opportunity to acquire valuable assets with dollars that steadily decrease in value. And that opportunity is presented better in the case of a home than in any other situation available to the ordinary citizen.

Suppose you could buy a large diamond and use borrowed money to do it and then repay the money with dirt. Or suppose you were a man dying of thirst and you could have cool, clear water just when you needed it and repay it with sand. That would be the approximate equivalent of what you do when you buy a home with a long-term mortgage.

Remember this and carve it on your dashboard.

1. Borrow valuable dollars
2. Buy a rapidly rising asset with the borrowed dollars
3. Pay back when the dollars are no longer valuable

That, in a nutshell, is buying a house in the era of continuous inflation.

Here's how it works. By definition, inflation means that your money is getting to be worth less and less, but also that you have more and more of it. For instance, although a dollar in 1979 buys only less than what 25 cents would have bought in 1942, many of us have more than four times as many dollars as we did then. Inflation, by its very meaning, says that we will all have vastly greater sums of dollars down the road of time, even though each dollar will be worth a lot less.

Also by definition, because we have fewer dollars now than we will have in the future, the dollars we have now are far more precious than the ones we will have in the future.

Remember that.

MONEYPOWER tells us that it is possible, indeed necessary, to buy something that will appreciate in value ahead of inflation and pay for it with precious borrowed dollars and then repay the loan with plentiful inflated dollars.

Let's try it in dollars and cents, just to see how very fine it is.

Let us take as our main characters in a small drama a young couple, Norman and Norma. They are thirty years old, and they want to buy a house. They are slightly above average in terms of their earnings and take home $300 a week, because they both work. As our story opens, Norman and Norma are renting an apartment for $300 a month.

They find a house that costs $60,000 and they love it. So they take their savings of $8,000, borrow $4,000 from Norma's parents, and buy the place.

The first year they have it, they pay one out of every three dollars for the house because they earn about $1,300 a month net and pay about $421 a month to service the mortgage. There is no doubt that any expenditure that takes one-third of all a young couple's money is a weighty one indeed. They are paying out very valuable dollars for that house.

But look what happens in five years: If Norman and Norma are like most couples, their income will rise in real terms by about 6 or 7 percent a year from the age of thirty to thirty-five. With 9 percent inflation added on—a low rate by today's standards—their incomes will rise by about 15 percent per year. At the end of five years, in round numbers, they will be earning about $2,800 a month net.

That means that they will have vastly more dollars, and yet their mortgage payments will be exactly the same. (If theirs is a flexible-rate mortgage, the payment will be higher, but not much. It could even be lower, but also, not much.) They will pay $421 out of $2,800—or one-seventh of all their dollars, which does not seem like much of a burden at all.

In ten years their income will have approximately doubled again, in dollar terms, to about $5,600 a month, and they will be spending only about 7½ percent of their income on their house.

They will be repaying valuable, scarce dollars with plentiful dollars, dollars that will be coming out of their ears.

Now bear in mind, those dollars will be worth a great deal less than they were when Norman and Norma used them to buy the house, *but the mortgage holder will still accept them as if they were just as valuabe as ever.*

In the interval, as Norman and Norma have watched the dollars get plentiful, their house will have risen sharply in value, far outperforming inflation. In five years, that $60,000 castle will be worth—taking the 1979 rate of appreciation of houses—$120,000 at least.

In ten years, that house, for which Norman and Norma are paying almost nothing, will be worth $240,000 at 1979 rates of inflation.

This is the most beautiful part of the MONEYPOWER strategy. As you pay less and less for that house because of inflation, your house gets to be worth more and more because of the same phenomenon.

And this analysis does not yet take into account the enormous tax savings that Norman and Norma would have enjoyed because of the deductibility feature of the interest on the mortgage.

The method that Norman and Norma used is exactly the same method that the great banks and speculators of the world use to make money on currency trades and complex arbitrage on world money markets. Norman and Norma are simply putting themselves in a position to be benefited—greatly—by the forces of inflation. They are putting themselves on top of the inflation wave, rather than under it.

But notice also what happens if this MONEYPOWER strategy is not followed. Suppose Norman and Norma had decided to stay in their apartment, save their money, and buy a house five years down the road.

- The price of houses would have risen far faster than the yield on their savings account
- They would have missed all the gain on the house, especially the money they made with other people's money
- Although their incomes would have risen dramatically in that five years, they would have completely missed out on the capital-gains income generated by the house at its preferentially lower rates

All of this, and all of the analysis that went before, might well be boiled down by saying that as soon as a young couple or a young person alone can even come close to buying a house he or she should buy a house with as little down payment as possible. If the payments are a burden at first, inflation is just about guaranteed to make them less of a burden in the future.

Rules promulgated in 1978 by various government agencies make the process easier even than it was before. Under flexible-term mortgages or graduated-payment mortgages, borrowers who qualify can pay smaller payments on the mortgage for the first five years of its life. Then, for the balance of the mortgage term, they will pay slightly higher payments than they otherwise would.

For example, if a couple have a $48,000 mortgage and owe $421 a month on it under normal circumstances, they might have a schedule under the graduated-payment-mortgage plan like this

Year of Mortgage	Payment
1–5	$340
6–30	$445

This is a plan that accentuates the whole MONEYPOWER concept of borrowing expensive dollars and paying back cheap dollars. Take advantage of it if you can.

A few further notes, explanatory and cautionary:

The more leveraged a property is, the better off the buyer is, in general. The simple reason is that the buyer will make money with borrowed money to add to what he makes on his own down payment, and the greater the amount of borrowed money, the greater the return on the investment of real money—and the greater the reliance the home buyer is placing on inflation to get those monthly payments down to an insignificant size.

Once again, it is often useful to look at the phenomenon in terms of dollars and cents.

Suppose Norman and Norma buy a $60,000 house with

only 10 percent down—which is usual in the case of a new development, rather than in the case of an older home. They will put down only $6,000 and they will borrow the rest. On a thirty-year, 10 percent mortgage, their monthly payments will be about $491. Obviously, that is a steep tab for a couple taking home about $1,300 a month, and, just as obviously, some belt-tightening is going to be in order. But, within five years, as their income swells through inflation and real gains in purchasing power to $2,800 a month net, they will be able to manage that monthly mortgage payment easily.

And, because of inflation, that house will have risen to be worth $97,000 at the end of the fifth year of ownership—taking a low figure of 10 percent for housing appreciation per year. The house will be worth $37,000 more than they paid for it, and they will have made over 600 percent on their initial investment of $6,000 (again, not counting the service of the mortgage, which, after all, bought them a place to live.)

In terms of following the principle of letting inflation bring their monthly payments into line, they will have done well also. By relying on more plentiful dollars in the future to relieve the early pressure of high monthly payments, Norman and Norma were able to buy a home even though they had only saved a small amount of money. They got all the advantages of inflation, starting at a much earlier stage of the inflationary spiral.

A key part of the strategy of borrowing valuable dollars and paying back cheap, plentiful dollars is to avoid doing just the opposite—borrowing expensive dollars and paying back even more expensive dollars.

The reader must be certain, or at least confident, that he will have more dollars in the future than he has now. For almost all working people in America, that is a safe bet. Even though rises in personal income tend to be less dramatic after age forty, inflation will raise the number of dollars in the weekly paycheck even if it lowers the purchasing power of those dollars. *(Remember—the mortgage holder is obligated to accept those dollars just as if they were worth the same as they were on the day the mortgage was signed.)*

But for one specific class of citizens there is a clear problem. Those who are now working and are about to retire must approach the whole situation differently. If you are now earning $500 a week and are about to retire, it is unlikely that you will continue to earn $500 a week—let alone more than $500 a week—after you retire. In fact, it is likely indeed that your weekly income will fall dramatically—unless you have an unusual pension plan or have most of your earnings from capital, rather than labor.

If you are about to retire, and if you have the prospect of fewer dollars coming in each week, you definitely cannot count on inflation to lower the burden of your mortgage payments. Buying a house still has many other useful and even marvelous benefits, but paying off scarce dollars with plentiful dollars is not one of them. (Retirees face extremely sensitive and special problems, which will be dealt with later in MONEYPOWER.)

But for most people, there is a virtual certainty that the weekly paycheck will be fatter—at least in normal dollars—as they move down the inflation road, and those plentiful dollars will be there to replace those scarce dollars.

There is one more advantage to buying a home that is more or less unique. Although some other investments have done far better than housing in beating inflation, at least on a short-term basis—specifically gold and foreign currencies—there are dramatic fluctuations in the prices of those commodities. Whereas gold buyers have done fabulously well on a long-term basis, even experienced gold bugs have been wiped out in the short term by price fluctuations.

Until quite recently, housing prices too were subject to dramatic fluctuations. When mortgage money dried up at banks and at savings and loan institutions, demand could not be fueled with money, and housing prices plummeted. Apparently, the most recent housing price declines, in 1966 and 1973–74, were caused by just this kind of crisis. (It is technically called disintermediation, which literally means that depositors withdraw their money from banks and savings and loan institutions to put it into instruments yielding higher returns, such as corporate debt instruments and government obligations.)

However, we are apparently entering a new era of immunity against drastic cutoffs of housing money. The government has allowed banks and savings and loan institutions to offer far more highly paying debt instruments to lenders—usually called T Bill Accounts or some variant—and depositors have tended to keep their money on deposit in the banks and S & L's. (These instruments are themselves interesting hedges and will be discussed later.)

Although mortgage money will be more plentiful some months than in other months, we can confidently look forward to an end of the complete exhaustion of money available for mortgages, at least for the foreseeable future. (If interest rates reach a level so high that banks and S & L's simply cannot follow them up, there could be yet another housing money cutoff. But the government has shown itself so eager to maintain the flow of funds into the housing market that a drought on the order of the 1966 or 1973–74 experience seems unlikely.)

All of this means that housing is not nearly as likely to be subject to the drastic ups and downs of the gold market or the international currency markets. Although you will never become rich overnight from the purchase of a house, you will rarely lose your shirt overnight either. A recession in house prices is a possibility, but all signs point to its being short-lived, to be succeeded by ever higher prices.

The demand for housing will continue to be fueled by ample mortgage money—barring interest-rate fever—and the rise in housing prices can be expected to move upward rapidly.

All is not a bed of roses, however, in buying and selling homes. The primary drawback is that in many parts of the country homes are a relatively illiquid commodity. That means they are difficult to sell quickly. It is not at all uncommon for a house to be on the market for several months before it sells.

What this means, very simply, is that if you were hoping to get your money out of the house in a hurry, you are likely to be disappointed. In this life, there are few transactions more frustrating and difficult than selling real estate. People who have needed the full value of their house in cash by a certain rapidly approaching date have all too often been cruelly disappointed.

In this respect almost any commodity or instrument traded on a public market is superior to real estate. There is simply nowhere near the liquidity in real estate that would be desirable.

Nevertheless, there are vital MONEYPOWER ways to safeguard yourself against the kind of cash crunch that can turn sweet dreams into 4 A.M. insomnia horror shows.

If you need money desperately—or even not desperately— and if the value of your home has gone up since the time you bought it (a virtual certainty), you can get some of that equity out through a second mortgage. A second mortgage is a loan secured by the value of your house but subordinated to the interests of the primary mortgage lender.

In most parts of the country these loans can be obtained through respectable financial institutions such as banks or occasional savings and loan institutions. The interest rate is generally far lower than for an unsecured personal loan, and the length of the loan is usually ten years or occasionally—but rarely—longer.

Encumbering your house with a second mortgage is a serious matter, because default on the loan can mean seizure of your house. But extremely few borrowers default, and for just that reason. Many people are willing to lose the use of their credit cards. Few are willing to lose the use of their homes. But if you are certain that you can make the payments, and if you genuinely need the money, a second trust deed can be just what the doctor ordered.

(The essence of the MONEYPOWER strategy is to borrow a great deal, but only to buy useful assets that will go up in value far faster than the rate of inflation. All other borrowings are in an inferior category.)

If you need the increased equity in your home so as to buy another home, and if you have not yet sold your present home, you can get a "swing loan" in many states to tide you over until you sell your present home. A swing loan is a short-term loan—usually for no more than 180 days—secured by a subordinated lien on your home. (Unless your house is completely paid off, in which case the swing-loan lender takes a primary lien. This is also true of the case above. If your house is completely paid off and you need money, you will not get a second mortgage, but a primary mortgage, in which the lender takes a primary lien on your home.) A swing loan is liquidated by the proceeds of the sale of your home, at which time the mortgage lien is removed.

In the case of either a refinancing of your home (usually a second mortgage) or a swing loan, there is usually a limit on just how much of the assessed value of your home the lender will lend. In California, the total indebtedness on a home may not exceed 80 percent of the assessed valuation. In many other states the total is slightly lower.

The point of all of this is simply that in a pinch there are often ways to get some of your money out of a home. (And in later chapters we will discuss just how useful it is to regularly refinance your property and get the equity out for various good uses.) But basically, in terms of buying and selling, a home is not a liquid asset.

That is a drawback, but, in terms of the MONEYPOWER strategy, it is about the only drawback there is to owning a home. You have to live somewhere. Why not make the place you live into a moneymaking machine?

Why not put yourself in a position to be enriched, rather than impoverished, by the currents of inflation?

Remember the key lesson of borrowing in the era of continuous inflation: Borrow valuable dollars and pay back cheap dollars. Then go buy a home.

Before the Normans and Normas of this world rush off to buy a house, there are certain preliminaries. The main one is to decide how much of a family's income should go into buying a home and servicing the mortgage. At one time there were hard and fast rules about these things. Lenders generally required that the mortgage payments for a house not exceed 25 percent of the family's adjusted net income—that is, income after legitimate tax deductions. For people with fluctuating weekly incomes, lenders generally insisted that a house cost no more than two and a half times the gross annual income of the buyer.

Those are still useful benchmarks. But they are no longer applied strictly by lenders nor should they be by borrowers. Lenders know that most people's incomes are not static. Inflation is a rising tide, however specious, which lifts all boats. Thus a lender can confidently expect that, as in our example, the borrowers for whom a loan payment is a sacrifice this year will find the payment negligible in the future.

The banks also know that their primary security is not the borrower's income, but the house. It too will rise in value as inflation rushes onward. And the bank that had a $60,000 asset as security in 1979 will have a $120,000 asset as security for a $44,000 loan in five years or less.

But in a sense, the bank's new flexibility about loans simply passes on the problem to the buyer. Even if a bank will lend on a house, it might still be wrong for the borrowers to borrow on it. In other words, the bank may cheerfully let you take on enormous payments that are too much for you.

There is a simple way to figure out the approximate amount you can afford to spend on monthly mortgage payments. Make a list of all of your other expenses besides housing, add 10 percent to it for errors, omissions, and next year's inflation, and then deduct it from your net pay. The remainder is what you can afford to pay.

If Norman and Norma cheat on their list and exaggerate their ability to pay, they will atone with sleepless nights. If they underestimate their ability to pay, they will have less house at work earning for them than they might have had.

Should the approach of drawing up a list prove too difficult, a buyer might well revert to the rule of taking one-fourth of his monthly net as his basis for monthly mortgage payments. But because of the certainty of inflation, he might go as far as to appropriate one-third of his net pay for housing if he feels confident about it.

Real-estate agents will often tell potential home buyers that they can spend half their income on housing because of inflation. But that goes too far. Only a family with a very large income can spend half on housing without lacking necessities. Be guided by good sense and MONEYPOWER strategy in making up your budget. Then you will enjoy beating inflation without suffering anxiety about paying for the groceries.

3

The Second Home:
Borrow, Borrow, Borrow

How do great captains of industry get to be great captains of industry? How do corporate wheelers and dealers get to be as rich as we would all like to be? Although mother and father's history might say that the Morgans and the Goulds and the Rockefellers did it by saving and frugality and hard work, the exact truth is quite different. People who get to be truly rich and important in the worlds of business and finance get that way by leverage of a rather special kind. They borrow money and buy part of a corporation, usually just enough to control the corporation. Then they use the first corporation's borrowing power to borrow money and use it to buy another company. They they use the combined borrowing power of the first two corporations to borrow enough money to buy control of yet another company. And so it goes. That is literally the exact way that the great conglomerates of the world were created.

In a nutshell, some brave man, a Harold Geneen or a Jay Gould or a John D. Rockefeller, used a small amount of money to gain control of a large amount of assets through the simple expedient of borrowing.

The sad truth is that most of us ordinary citizens are not

psychologically or intellectually equipped to duplicate the feats of the great corporate chiefs of American history. But we can certainly learn from their example. In fact, making good use of their examples is an essential part of the MONEYPOWER strategy.

It is possible for almost any gainfully employed adult in America to obtain control of a significant amount of assets that will rise in value far faster than inflation with only a small amount of his own money. The vehicles for this marvelous accomplishment are several, but the preferred one is once again the single-family home.

To understand just how it works and why, we might begin by observing that the year of the writing of this book, 1979, is also the year in which, for the first time, over 50 million families in America owned their own homes. Those families have obviously no particular need of the MONEYPOWER advice to get their own homes. But they do need to understand why owning their own homes is a little like owning a small corporation that will be the base of their financial empires.

Let us take the hypothetical Jones family, headed by John Jones, a sales manager in Los Angeles for a firm selling rubber goods. John is forty years old. Back in 1968, John bought a house in Glendale, a suburb of Los Angeles, for $30,000. Since then, the house has risen in value to become worth $120,000. John originally had a mortgage of $24,000, which has now been reduced to $20,000 outstanding. The mortgage is at 6 percent, a common amount in 1968.

John's monthly payments on the mortgage are $143.90, which was a strain back in 1968 when he was earning $12,000 a year; but now that he is earning $38,000, the payment is almost unnoticeably small. He has extra money to spend on MONEYPOWER inflation-beating strategies. He is sick of being victimized by inflation.

John is a man with insight and foresight, and he does not want to see inflation ruin his life. Instead, he wants to use his money to make inflation work *for* him. John also loves his neighborhood. His children and his wife have good friends there, and he is not eager to move.

Also, John loves the desert. He finds the clean, dry air bracing, and his wife loves to lie in the sun and read English detective stories.

First move: John decides to buy a condominium in the desert. He finds one that he likes for $60,000. Because it is a second home, he will have to pay 25 percent down and finance the rest. John happens to have about $15,000 in his savings account, but he wants to keep some of it there so that he can have cash in case of emergency.

Second move: John decides to refinance his house so that he can have the money for the down payment on his desert condo. He goes to the bank and obtains a second trust deed loan on his Glendale house in the amount of $15,000. It is a ten-year loan at 12 percent interest. The monthly payment is $215.21.

Third move: John buys the desert condominium. He puts down the $15,000 he has obtained from the second trust deed on his house—making certain that if he is asked on any form, he explains the origin of the money—and borrows $45,000 for the rest of the payment. His $45,000 mortgage is for thirty years at 10 percent interest. His monthly payment is $394.91. Counting his monthly payment on the second mortgage on his Glendale house, his monthly payments on his new house are $610.

Fourth move: John rents the condominium to families from Los Angeles or anywhere else who want to spend a few days in the sun while it is cold and rainy wherever they are. He can rent the condo for $65 a night, and he finds that he can rent it for about seventy-five nights the first year. He realizes $4,875 in rentals in the first year, of which he has to pay an agent 15 percent, leaving him with a net of $4,143.75.

Obviously, that rental does not even come close to covering

John's mortgage costs on the property, which are $7,320 a year, not to mention his taxes and condominium fees, which are probably another $1,500 a year.

John is putting about $4,700 of his own money into the property each year, or so it would seem. But look more closely. That condo is not costing John money. It is coining money for him.

First, in the first few years almost all of the money that John pays for mortgage payments is tax deductible. Let us assume that John is in the 30 percent marginal bracket for state and federal taxes. That means his *real,* after-tax costs of the yearly mortgage amount plus the taxes and condo fees are about $3,600 a year.

Second, unless a plague of giant, atomic mutant ants were to wipe out Palm Springs, or unless people stopped liking sunshine, we might assume that the value of the desert property would rise by at least 15 percent per year, which is what property in that area has been doing recently. That means the house is worth, at the end of the first year, $69,000. Taking into account the capital-gains rate for a man in John's bracket, John has made about $7,400 on that house in the first year. Subtracting the real, after-tax loss on rentals, John has made $3,800 in the first year—on an out-of-pocket investment of absolutely *zero.* He borrowed every penny.

But it gets even better than that. Each year the rentals will go up, as inflation goes up, and yet John's fixed costs, primarily the mortgage, will remain almost entirely stable. It is likely that in three years he will break even on the house solely in terms of rentals, not counting the capital gains!

Even if the rate of appreciation in desert real estate drops dramatically, say to 10 percent per year, John will still have a condo worth $83,500 at the end of the third year. In the fourth year, he will have $8,350 of capital-gains income alone— after he has paid for all his maintenance expenses by means of the rents.

If all the mathematics leaves you dizzy, you need only remember that John

1. Bought the house with borrowed money
2. Paid for most of it with the rents of other people
3. Made money on it from the very first year because of the capital gains
4. Has a vacation home to enjoy.

John has done the exact equivalent of what the captains of industry do. He has parlayed a small stake of his own money—the equity in his Glendale home—into a large earning asset—in John's case it is real estate—without having to go through the tedious and impossible task of saving for years.

But John is far from finished. He has used the inflationary increase in value of his Glendale home to generate still more income by taking some of that increased value and buying the desert home. That is MONEYPOWER in action. Now let us see what John does next.

Let us remember that it is now four years since John mortgaged his home in Glendale for a second time. It is, let us imagine, 1982. That home in Glendale is now worth $150,000 (a conservative estimate, considering the way things have been going). John wants to get still more property, and so he refinances his home in Glendale yet again. That home is growing money, and John wants to take some out of the rafters and beams and use it to buy things.

First Move: John goes to his bank and arranges to refinance his house. He does not refinance all of it, because he wants to hold on to that 6 percent mortgage as long as he can. Instead, he arranges for a new second trust deed. This time the loan is for $50,000. (Remember that in California, where John lives, he can borrow up to 80 percent of the total value of the home, so he is still well below that limit.) The loan is for ten years at 12 percent. The monthly payment is $717.36. John uses $12,000 of the proceeds (approximately) to pay off the prior second mortgage, leaving him with a balance for ready use of $38,000. (Or he can refinance the desert home.)

Second Move: John buys another house right in Los Angeles, not for his own use, but strictly as a rental. He uses most of the proceeds of his second trust on the Glendale house for the down payment and the rest for repairs and renovations.

But before the eyes of the reader glaze over, we can forego all the mathematics of the desert condo example. All we need to know is that the rental property will almost certainly not pay its way in terms of paying off the mortgage, but that it will almost certainly start making money for the kindly John right away because of capital gains. It will also yield important deductions from tax income for depreciation and maintenance as a tax matter.

And the reason it will start making money for John immediately is simply that the rate of inflation in housing prices is so very far ahead of all the other costs associated with owning a home—especially the cost of borrowing.

Also, just as in the case of the desert condo operation, John's rentals will rise rapidly, as inflation pulls them up too, while his costs, primarily servicing the mortgage, will remain more or less constant. Soon John's rental property in Los Angeles will yield both ordinary and capital-gains income.

That is, within a few years, John's rents will exceed his yearly costs of maintaining the residence, including paying off the mortgage. He will have ordinary income from the rental property, just as if he owned a bond or had a certificate of deposit.

In addition, John will continue to realize his capital-gains income from the house. The situation is very much the same as if John could

1. Buy a stock that yielded a good dividend with borrowed money
2. Watch the stock go up rapidly
3. Pay off the loan with inflated money that was plentiful and easy to come by

4. Be certain that the stock would not be subject to wild fluctuations in price
5. Borrow against the stock to buy still more stock with the same wonderful characteristics as the first stock

Unfortunately, there is no such stock. But there are houses. John can repeat the operation of borrowing on the equity in his properties to buy still more rental property as often as he

1. Finds a property that offers him steady and steadily rising rental income, eventually and rapidly reaching a level that pays for maintenance of the property
2. Can afford to carry the operating and mortgage financing costs of the property until it becomes self-supporting
3. Believes that the inflationary situation is such that the property will rise in value significantly faster than the rate of inflation

Each of these is a crucial prerequisite. John will be buying himself only grief if he has to continually underwrite part of the rental property, without ever having the prospect that the property will—on a cash basis—become self-supporting. (If John uses the property as a second or third home and realizes psychic enjoyment from it, he might consider that he should be out of pocket something and that the property need not be self-supporting from the rental payments.)

This analysis assumes that John will frequently use the desert home for his family's enjoyment. If he does, he cannot treat it entirely as a business asset and cannot deduct as much depreciation on the house as if he did not use it.

Certainly John could depreciate the rental property he bought back in town. John's expenses associated with the house could also be deducted—painting, accounting, plumbing, and so forth. Again, as with the desert condo, this lowers the tax bite, and thus lowers the burden of maintaining the property. By the same token, these tax advantages increase the difference between the yearly cost of maintaining the property and the yearly increase in value of the property.

Even when the rents rise to the point where the owner, John Jones, is making significant ordinary rental income, John can count on lowering his taxes a great deal by deducting every niggling item of expense. The depreciation deduction is a special kind of manna. It allows John to act as if his property were becoming less valuable, when everyone knows it is becoming more valuable (although at some point far down the road, if John is careless, that benefit can be recaptured by the IRS).

Still, the road is not all roses.

If John cannot afford to keep up the payments on the property and must constantly worry about where he will find the money to maintain the house while he waits for its capital-gains value to materialize in cash, he will have made a major mistake. There is a great deal of sense to stretching your resources a bit to put yourself in the way of getting rich from inflation. There is no sense at all to driving yourself crazy over it. No investment yet discovered is worth anguish and sleepless nights. It is far better to lose some of your savings to the ravages of inflation than to lose your good health and peace of mind by worrying about meeting mortgage payments with money you do not have.

There is absolutely no point at all to buying a house or other property unless you believe it will give a generous capital gain—a gain that is better than you could have gotten from bonds or certificates of deposit and better than the rate of inflation.

But, with some planning and foresight, those conditions can be met, and the reader and John will have the inflation-beating ball rolling along: Taking inflation-generated equity out of house number one, using it to buy house number two, waiting for the inflation-generated equity in house number two to increase, then taking it out to buy yet another house, and repeating the process until some as yet unknown fate comes along to end the inflationary process.

Using real estate paid for with borrowed money to generate large capital gains is exactly analogous to what corporate wheeler-dealers do to create giant industrial empires. Not only is the real-estate avenue the best avenue yet arrived at for taking advantage of inflation, but for the average citizen it is the *only* means whereby he can secure large amounts of borrowed capital on which he can get large returns, returns greater than the rate of inflation without dramatic price fluctuations.

And again, because it bears repeating endlessly, the reason he can get those enormous returns is that he makes money not only on his down payment, but also on all the money he borrowed.

Think of this situation. Five of your neighbors line up and tell you that in addition to your own wages, you will henceforth take 20 percent of their wages. You would soon find yourself far out in front of inflation.

It is exactly the same with mortgages on real property. You are making money not only on the money you put down, but on all the bank's (or S & L's) money, which has been generously lent to you at rates so low that you make money while the depositors see their savings waste away, year by year.

A further note on why the MONEYPOWER strategy of buying single-family homes or condos is right for our times. Many, many people have gotten rich from buying and renting multi-unit dwellings—apartment houses—in our time. It is a staple way for immigrants and other determined people to raise themselves from the Woolworth to the Saks level in two generations.

Recently, however, a problem has arisen in connection with that strategy. It is called rent control. Many of our largest municipalities have adopted laws limiting the rents that can be charged for rental units in multi-unit buildings. In some cities the legal limits are so low that it is simply impossible to come close to breaking even on a cash basis with those buildings. The prices of the apartment buildings are too high and the rentals far too low to pay for servicing mortgages, let alone the other costs of upkeep.

Thus, the multi-unit owner must hope for substantial increases in the capital value of his building to make money. Sometimes those increases come and sometimes they do not. When a city adopts rent-control ordinances, it takes a while for the permanence of the measure to sink in to prospective buyers. But once the market for apartment houses realizes that few rent-control laws are ever abolished, and few rises are ever allowed under those laws, the prices of multi-unit dwellings stay low for some time, and prospects for raising the rental revenue from the buildings go a-glimmering.

Despite the mass of evidence that rent-control laws do not work but instead ravage the rental housing market for renters as well as landlords, rent-control laws have been spreading rapidly. Any sudden bad economic news can bring them on swiftly, and then they stay in force forever. And, again, that drastically harms prospects for a good capital gain.

MONEYPOWER research has found that rent controls are almost never applied to single-family rental units—that is, houses or condos owned by a private citizen that are not part of a multi-unit building. In an era of expanding government tampering with the economic system, this is a heavy weight on the side of buying single units to keep ahead of inflation.

4

How and Why It
Works: Arbitrage

As the preceding chapters have shown, housing is a superb tool to keep yourself far ahead of inflation. It is important to know the financial and social dynamics that have made housing such a magnificent hedge against inflation so that if a change in any of those forces appears upon the horizon, we can know how to react to pursue optimal MONEYPOWER stragegy.

All of what MONEYPOWER teaches about housing comes under the categories of arbitrage and second-level analysis. And if those terms sound somewhat arcane, it is well worth your while to learn something about them.

Arbitrage is basically the trading of different assets for each other when one or more of those assets has become overpriced in terms of the other assets. To take a very simple example of classical arbitrage, imagine a wealthy man with millions of dollars to play with. He sees that on a certain day, on the New York currency markets, one dollar is trading for .5 British pounds. But he sees that in the London currency market, the dollar is trading for .48 British pounds. In other words, the dollar is worth less in London than in New York. So Mr. X., the rich gentleman, buys 1 million British pounds with dollars in New York. For them, he pays $2 million.

He then electronically takes his 1 million pounds to London and sells them for dollars. Because a dollar is worth less in London, our friend gets more dollars for his pounds. In fact, he gets about $83,000 more than his original $2 million investment. Usually, the differences in currency prices among different markets are far less pronounced than in the example. Moreover, the differences are often among several different currencies. A speculator might trade dollars for Deutsche marks in Frankfurt, D-marks for Swiss francs in Zurich, and then Swiss francs back into dollars in New York.

Or the currency trade might involve speculation in currencies, metals, and shares of companies. For instance, a trader might trade dollars into pounds in New York, then use the pounds to buy gold in Tokyo, and then use the gold to buy Deutsche marks in Singapore, and then use the Deutsche marks to buy dollars in New York.

Needless to say, the heavy traders in this kind of market use advanced electronic equipment to keep up with the frantic movements of assets on markets around the world. But basically what they do is simply buy something that is valued excessively high and then trade it back into the basic currency.

And that is exactly what the MONEYPOWER strategy is to beat inflation. Every citizen who wants to keep up with inflation and get ahead of it will become an arbitrageur on a small scale. He will learn to trade his dollars for something that he can then trade back for a much larger amount of dollars. And the main asset he can use for this kind of down-home arbitrage is a twofold commodity—residential single-family homes *and the low down payment, long-term form of financing that makes them so effective at beating inflation.*

The MONEYPOWER strategy on houses is several kinds of arbitrage all rolled into one.

First, it is turning dollars into houses and then back into dollars. A man who buys a house puts his dollars into a little piece of land, building materials, and construction costs. He is betting that within a reasonable amount of time, he can convert them back into far more dollars than he originally put into them. Notice that the man who converted dollars into pounds and then back into dollars made only about 4 percent profit. He customarily makes it in the space of about thirty seconds, however. The man who arbitrages from dollars into houses and then back into dollars should make a far greater percent, but over a period of years.

The historical evidence available tells us that the man who expects to convert the components of a house back into dollars that have grown numerous at a rate faster than the rate of inflation will rarely be disappointed. The price of housing— as we have learned in recent years—regularly keeps far ahead of the rate of inflation. Betting on houses as a form of arbitrage is not a sure thing, as nothing is, but at least the weight of history is on the side of the home buyer.

The second way that buying a house is like arbitrage is in its financing component. The uniquely wonderful American way of financing homes allows the home buyer to bet on the price rise of homes with someone else's money, *and thereby to greatly lower his own cost and greatly magnify his own gains.*

As we have seen, buying a house with borrowed money is like getting a gift from the bank. You are able to use the depositors' money and pay less for its use than you make with it. You are thus able to arbitrage with borrowed money. Imagine in the example about the wealthy man who speculated on dollars and pounds that the man had borrowed the money for the speculation, so that he did not have to put up any of his own money at all. Then imagine that he did not even have to be wealthy in the first place. That would be similar to the case of the man who buys a home with a long-term mortgage.

When you use a bank or an S & L to finance your house purchase, you are, in fact, doing even better than getting someone to lend you money for a currency arbitrage. The reason is that when you repay the loan you are paying off with dollars that are substantially less valuable than when you borrowed them. If the man in the currency arbitrage did not have to pay back his imaginary loan for several years, and then had to pay back only a half or a third of what he had borrowed, then he would be a great deal like the happy homeowner. (Bear in mind that "homeowner" or "home buyer," in MONEY-POWER, refers to people who follow the best MONEYPOWER strategy of buying their own primary residences and then buying still other houses.)

The third way in which buying houses is like arbitrage against inflation is that it is essentially taking an option that the dollar will be worth less plotted against time. With borrowed money, you are betting that the rate of inflation will continue to rise at a more rapid rate than the interest cost and at a rate more rapid—taking into account the financing feature—than any other competitive, easily acquired asset.

If the currency speculator in the example could have bought an option on inflation, he would be like the home buyer. If, instead of buying dollars and then pounds and then dollars again, he had bought dollars, then some hypothetical currency that would move in the same direction as inflation but much faster, and then converted those hypothetical currencies into dollars—well, just call that hypothetical currency "houses" and you have the idea.

The man who follows the MONEYPOWER strategy to buy houses is following a plan every bit as sophisticated as the currency speculator, and every bit as intelligent—and far more likely to succeed.

Now the cautious reader may say, as he should, "There is no such thing as a free lunch. How can it be that people can make money on housing for all eternity? The science of economics tells us that the returns on different forms of investment tend to level off and be in equilibrium. Why doesn't this happen in housing? Why isn't the return on housing basically the same as the return on savings accounts?"

Those are good questions. They illustrate the crucial necessity of looking at things beyond the surface level. In other words, second-order analysis is always the best kind.

To take the questions as the cautious reader put them, "How can it be that people can make money on housing for all eternity?" Simply put, people did not make money on housing for all eternity. For most of recorded eternity, housing prices fluctuated. They rose and fell, along with the prices of everything else. When there were boom times, real-estate prices rose. When there were bad times, real-estate prices collapsed.

Even in more recent times, such as that part of eternity that has passed since World War II, there have been marked fluctuations in the prices of housing. When there were bad times, demand fell off and prices fell. Sometimes the market would get overbuilt, and overhanging supply would depress prices. Most recently of all, when the government tried to stop inflation, the Federal Reserve Board cut down on the supply of money, and mortgage funds dried up. The resulting lack of demand often led to sharp declines in housing prices.

Even while prices were generally rising in the postwar period, even rising sharply, there were periods of decline. But there have been fundamental changes in construction, finance, and government intervention in the economy in recent years. They have brought about an entirely new situation in the home-buying market.

Several factors are at work. All of them have made for far better and more stable conditions for the home buyer.

First, the government has allowed the creation of new financial instruments that allow banks and savings and loans to attract money from depositors even at times when interest rates are skyrocketing and the money supply is sluggish. As many people remember, S & L's, the prime lenders on homes, once were allowed to pay only passbook interest on deposits.

When interest rates rose on Treasury bills, bank certificates of deposit, and corporate paper, depositors withdrew their money from S & L's and put it in those higher yielding places.

Now, as anyone who watches television knows, S & L's can offer depositors six-month certificates paying the rate on Treasury bills. This has not only slowed outflows during the recent period of "high" interest rates, but has actually improved S & L deposit inflows. Banks have done the same thing and have attracted money as well. In addition, banks and S & L's can sell (or "rediscount") mortgage debt to various federal instrumentalities to obtain money to make new loans.

The times when potential home buyers simply could not find mortgage money anywhere are gone. A potential buyer may still have to go from Citizens to Home to First National to Valley Federal to get his mortgage, but he will get it somewhere.

A major source of falloff in demand for housing has been eliminated. If buyers can get money to buy, drastic drops in demand for housing will be far less likely.

A second major change in the economic situation relative to houses is this: Although recessions will still come and go, the pent-up demand for housing is apparently so strong that even generalized lower levels of economic activity do not affect housing prices as much as they did at one time. Through the last major recession—1974–75—housing demand fell off, but not nearly as much as one might have expected.

The third major change in the economy that benefits housing is that the government has become acutely aware of just how important the residential construction industry is. Some congressional districts may not have oilmen or natural-gas producers, but every district has a few builders who are good friends of the congressman. They get on the long-distance phone to Washington in a big hurry when they see a housing slowdown coming. They tell their pal, the Member of Congress, that if the government keeps squeezing up interest rates, there will be a lot of unhappy contributors and a lot of unemployed hod carriers looking for new political faces. So the government simply will not let residential construction drop precipitously. And the same measures that boost new residential construction—namely making ample mortgage money available—also keep the secondary home market lively.

All of those measures act on the demand side. There is also one big help to the home buyer on the supply side. For a variety of reasons, building a house has become incredibly time consuming. The National Association of Home Builders recently reported that the construction of a home—from conception to finished product—took six months ten years ago and takes more than two years in 1978.

There are new, more complicated rules and regulations in building codes all over the country. These codes serve mainly to insure that building a house will require immense amounts of union labor. They also assure that it will take a long time to finish each house.

Environmental regulations to protect the field mice and the wild grasses and other exotica all over America have made home building into a treacherous minefield of difficulties. At any stage, an earnest bureaucrat can pigeonhole a project forever. A hippie in a three-piece suit, fresh out of law school, can pick apart a builder's proposal until the builder and his plans simply mildew from disuse.

Zoning regulations have become as complicated as environmental-impact statements. In every part of the country zoning officials sit to pass judgment upon whether or not any building is compatible with the zoners' ideas of how the world should be run. Even if the zoning officials do not have their hands out, the normal delays that occur when any bureaucrat is asked to do anything useful can hold up a house for months if not years.

Add to that the growing scarcity of decent land, the impossibility of finding workers who will do any work with any consistency, the Kafkaesque difficulties in getting any kind of materials delivered, and you have a good idea of why it now takes so long to build a house.

The result—a chronic shortage of supply for houses. Supply hardly ever catches up with demand except during the worst of housing slumps, as in 1974. And then, when the recession is over, the demand rebounds so fast that we have fantastic run-ups in price, as supply cannot nearly keep pace.

And this, in fact, is exactly the reason why the cautious reader's question about housing coming into equilibrium is unrealistic. Yes, in the ideal world, as prices for housing rose, more housing would be supplied, and then the supply would depress the price, and so all disequilibriums in price movements would end. Houses would, in this ideal economist's world, come down in price so that homeowners would not continue to make fantastic profits on them.

But in the ideal economist's world, a nineteen-year-old drunk who knows how to attach pipes to each other and is called a plumber would work as many hours as he could at $30 an hour instead of soaking up beers at a tavern. Adam Smith never contemplated a world in which people simply will not work.

Today, the "frictional" problems in supply—that is, workers who will not work and the dead hand of the bureaucracy—make it impossible that housing will ever be in equilibrium. The government can *and does* keep up demand by flooding the banks and S & L's with money—but it takes forever for the construction industry to meet the demand. Thus we have what should be impossible in the ideal world—chronic shortage and chronic disequilibrium in the direction of high prices.

This is all important to keep in mind for this reason: If something ever happens to allow housing to be manufactured quickly, then part of the reason why houses are such a fine inflation hedge will come to an end. If the alert MONEYPOWER investor ever reads that split-level brick houses can be mass-produced in Taiwan and shipped to America, he should get out of the housing market fast.

There should be similar vigilance on the demand side. If, by some miracle of prudence and foresight, the American people ever elect a President and a Congress who will truly lower the boom on inflation even if it means a severe, prolonged recession, then the dynamics of the supply side will change.

Should the government start soaking up excess funds in the economy instead of generating more, the banks and S & L's will soon find themselves without any money to lend for a lengthy period, and the housing market will dry up seriously. The careful MONEYPOWER investor should be aware that such a possibility exists, however remote. (And the possibility is remote indeed. Although many politicians like to campaign against inflation, *no* politicians like to campaign on a program of high unemployment, low profits, and hard times.)

In the event that the government plunges the economy into prolonged recession, the prospect will also exist that tomorrow's dollars will be more valuable instead of less valuable. If there is high unemployment, an end of easy pay raises, and begging in the streets, wage earners cannot comfortably expect to take in far more dollars one year than they did the year before. That means that they should beware entangling themselves with heavy debt charges.

But all of this speculation on whether the United States will return to an administration of Draconian strictness in fighting inflation is somewhat like speculating about what would have happened if Stalin had become a Baptist. It is interesting, but we are unlikely to find out.

So far, even while the President and Congress have said that *this time* (1979) they really mean it, and that this time they will really hold the nation's monetary feet to the fire, inflation roars on at full speed. The banks and savings and loans can get plenty of money. Interest rates, which look high by historical standards, are quite low.

And even as this is written, while newspapers scream about skyrocketing interest rates of 11 and 12 percent, the alert MONEYPOWER investor will realize that in an era where inflation of 10 percent a year overall can be expected, 11 and 12 percent interest rates are far lower than a 4 percent rate in an era of price stability.

If housing is rising at 10 to 15 percent per year in price, an interest rate of 10⅝ percent is not high. It is free.

So one might sensibly conclude that if interest rates during a government squeeze on money are barely positive (barely above the rate of inflation), the government is not truly serious about cracking the whip over inflation. At least not yet.

(An interesting historic parallel: During the most fevered days of the Weimar inflation of 1923, when prices were doubling every few hours, the Weimar government still made loans to businesses for capital expansion at rates of about 70 percent interest per year. This rate, which was perhaps one ten-thousandth of the true rate of inflation, was considered "high" by historic standards, since it had only recently been raised from 6 percent.)

Second-order analysis is really nothing more than looking below the surface level of things. Notice that the economy has changed. Notice that housing is a far more stable industry than it was. Notice that demand is constantly stimulated and supply—in housing—is constantly suppressed. Notice that even while the government proclaims a war against inflation, interest rates are still ridiculously low.

Notice that the reason you make so much money on houses is because you make money on borrowed money as well as your own money. Notice that the income-tax laws are all on your side.

And then, after you have noticed all of those things, notice that it is possible—however unlikely for a prolonged period—that these things will change. And when they do change, get ready for some rethinking.

5

Liquidation: When, and
How to Sell

So far there is something missing from the MONEYPOWER advice on buying houses to keep up with and beat inflation. The alert reader will notice that while the preceding chapters have told him something about how to acquire real estate worth a great deal of money, nothing has been said about converting that real estate into actual cash.

At what point is it smart to liquidate the investments in real property and convert them into money in the bank?

That is a highly subjective question. In fact, MONEYPOWER recognizes no absolute answer. If inflation continues forever, and if the price of houses continues to outpace inflation—when considered along with the enormous advantages of borrowing to buy them—it would be sensible to continue buying and holding the houses forever.

Two problems occur, however, that might cause a problem with holding and buying indefinitely. First, sometimes people need actual cash on hand, instead of cash in the illiquid form of real estate, and sometimes people find that inflation comes to an end.

And these are the two primary definitions of the right times to liquidate your housing investment:

1. If you need money badly—and will not be able to repay it
2. If inflation seems to be slowing down drastically

Generally, if a man with a good job needs a sudden transfusion of money, and if he feels certain that he will continue to be employed gainfully, then he can borrow on the equity in his real property and repay the loan over a long period. Sometimes, however, people retire or go into convalescence or simply need money and see no reasonable prospect of paying it back. In those cases it is time to liquidate some of the real property that MONEYPOWER has helped you acquire.

The final end of the MONEYPOWER strategy, after all, is not to acquire a lot of property so that you can brag about it to your neighbors. The goal is to take you financially ahead of inflation, so that you will not have to fear a pauper's grave once inflation has made your money worthless. But once MONEYPOWER has put you well ahead of the inflationary rat race, you should think of the money in your property as something to be used as needed. It is not a sacred or inviolable trust. It is an emergency ration, to be consumed as necessary.

All of your efforts and sacrifice to acquire real assets will be undone if you do not liquidate those assets at some time when you need money. The assets have no reason for being except to aid the owner. They will be inanimate mockeries if you have worked to build them up and then let them stand inviolate while you suffer privation.

The other time to liquidate is when you see signs that inflation is coming to an end. MONEYPOWER strategy is premised on the easily observed fact that inflation is not coming to an end any time soon. But at some point, however distant, inflation will come to an end for a significant period. The early warning signals of that event will be described in a later chapter. All that you must realize is that if the rate of inflation in housing does peter out—not for just a few months or a year, but for the foreseeable future, the ambitious real-estate acquirer will be left with a problem: While his costs will remain constant, the value of his property will stop rising rapidly, and may even fall. Suddenly the equation that made homeownership so profitable—the low cost of acquisition and maintenance, high selling price—will be reversed.

Bear in mind that the reason housing prices rise rapidly is because people anticipate still higher prices in the future. If people stop anticipating still higher prices in the future, current prices will not rise, at least not as much, and interest rates may well fall.

Again, such a sustained and drastic falloff in inflation is in the distant future, but it is something to be kept in the back of your mind.

If you need the money and it is not sensible to borrow, and if you believe inflation is coming to an end—these are the two times to liquidate. But there is a major difference between the strategies to follow in each case.

In the first case, the real-estate owner should sell off only what he needs. He should retain the rest and let it keep outperforming inflation and improving his net worth. Remember, in inflationary times, it is unlikely that any other asset will appreciate so rapidly and so steadily.

In the second case, if the inflationary whirlwind should stop blowing, the property owner should liquidate everything. The opportunity for making money in real estate will have passed for a while. The proceeds of all those liquidations should be placed in investments more suitable for periods of price stability—bonds, certificates of deposit, and other such fixed-income instruments.

But remember, there are many, many promises that inflation will be halted but almost no halts. There must be solid, virtually incontrovertible evidence that inflation is at an end, and even then MONEYPOWER would advise skepticism, before the alert reader should be convinced that the era of inflation is at an end. It may well not end in the lifetime of many people reading this book.

6

Farming: A Rich Man's Club

There is one type of real estate that is a special case of the MONEYPOWER strategy. This type of real estate appears to be almost certainly the best kind of real estate to buy or own for capital appreciation and is almost certainly the most difficult to get your hands on and keep. It is called farmland. But there is a catch.

Farming is about the most difficult and unrewarding kind of work a man can do in America circa 1979. It involves unremitting toil in bad weather, dirt, and noise. An emergency can take the farmer away from his hearth at any moment. He is totally subject to the whims of nature in a way unheard of for any other occupation.

Moreover, if by luck and planning and hard work a farmer makes a good living one year, the government stands ready to take it away from him the next year. For example, if a beef rancher sees prices go up and gets ready to slaughter some of his herd, the next thing he hears is that the President has announced that the United States will import 100 million pounds of Australian beef. Down go the prices.

Or if a wheat rancher comes in with a particularly good crop, he can face the same kinds of troubles. The President can refuse to allow the wheat to be exported to Russia, and suddenly the rancher is up against full Harvestores and no place to sell the wheat.

But there is a solid-gold lining. Although farming is a pain in the neck, owning farmland is about the best occupation in the world next to owning Kuwait. The rise in the price of American farmland in the postwar period has been nothing short of stupendous. For more than a decade, farmland has risen—on an average nationwide basis—at a rate of more than 20 percent per year, compounded.

That means that farmland costing $300 an acre back on January 1, 1968, will rise to more than $2,900 an acre on May 15, 1979. The value of the land doubles about every forty-five months! It is a price rise that is staggering even by comparison with the rise in the price of single-family houses.

Small wonder that the most active Rolls-Royce agency in the world is in Nebraska. Small wonder that most of the millionaires in this country are farmers.

Consider the farmer who right after World War II had a 2,000-acre place in the middle of Wyoming that was good for maybe $25 an acre. Now he is a multimillionaire. One of the truly astonishing revelations of modern life is to attend a meeting of the farmers in any midwestern or western state. There are almost no people present who are not millionaires.

Small wonder that wealthy Europeans, Arabs, and Japanese are buying American farmland as fast as they can. It is a long way from any guerrilla movements. It grows a cash return every year. It is not going anywhere. And it is unlikely to be nationalized.

Bear in mind that those wealthy foreigners can buy gold or oil leases or debt instruments denominated in Deutsche marks. They can buy anything. They are betting that U.S. farmland is about as good an investment as there is.

The value of farmland rises almost completely irrespective of current or near-term prices for United States farm commodities. Prime soybean land rose as much—or almost as much—before the great soybean price rises of 1971, '72, and '73 as during and afterward.

The attraction of farmland for both Americans and foreigners is its security, apparently, plus the distant hope of much larger crop prices.

Farmland is about the best thing to own to beat inflation. It rises in value so fast that it hardly even sees inflation behind it. Its major problem is that it is extremely difficult for the ordinary citizen to acquire—except perhaps through inheritance.

But there is, once again, a catch. Basically, the problem is with the financing. There is simply no equivalent of home finance in the farmland market. Forget about 10 or 20 percent down and thirty years to pay. The standard form of purchase for a farm is all cash. That's right. All cash.

Occasionally, the seller will finance the purchase. If he does that, he does it by taking 29 percent down and taking the rest over ten years in most cases. The laws of federal income tax allow a farmer to take his capital gains over a long period and pay the tax over a similarly long period if he spreads out the period of payment and takes no more than 29 percent in cash. That is an incentive in some cases.

In a few cases, a bank near the farm will lend on the property. But a bank will almost never lend more than 50 percent of the price, and the repayment term is usually quite short. It is rarely more than five years. Insurance companies will sometimes lend on truly enormous farms and ranches, but they will rarely finance more than 50 percent. And the places they will even consider financing are almost always multimillion-dollar properties in any event. Federal agencies will lend, but only to bona fide farmers—not to speculators.

(Remember that with farm prices the way they are, it does not take the King Ranch to make a million-dollar property. Almost any working ranch of economical size is a million-dollar ranch unless it is in some particularly barren area.)

Sometimes a farmer will consider an exchange of his valuable appreciated property for an equivalently valuable piece of income property. There is value for both parties to such a deal.

Federal tax laws allow tax-free exchanges of appreciated property. This means both parties escape taxation on the transaction, which can mean a very considerable savings.

The farmer gets a higher income relative to the capital investment when he takes the apartment house or office building, and the income property owner gets far faster capital gains when he takes the farm. Presumably, each gets what he wants. (The MONEYPOWER strategy would always favor taking the capital gains, which will put the investor more consistently ahead of inflation than will almost any kind of ordinary income.)

These facts about farms are interesting and curious, but they are fundamentally of only small help to the MONEYPOWER investor. There is simply no easy way to finance farmland, and this lack usually places it out of the reach of all but the most-well-heeled investors.

Occasionally, however, farms and ranches are bought by groups of investors who pool their resources to buy a property that no member of the group could possibly afford alone. For instance, if there is a farm for sale for $250,000, and if the owner will take 30 percent down, then each investor of a group of five might put up $15,000 for the total down payment of $75,000.

Of course, each member of the group will then also put down on paper a pledge to pay his share of the monthly service on the mortgage and other upkeep on the property. Such an agreement, sometimes called a syndication, should be drawn up by a lawyer in your area. Legal rules as to how much liability each owner must and should incur differ from area to area, and professional legal advice is a must for such a transaction.

A successful syndication can make money for all of the people involved in it. For example, if the farm is worth $250,000 and rises in value by 18 percent a year (to take a conservative estimate), and if the loan is for a ten-year period at 9 percent interest, then at the end of the first year, the farm will be worth $295,000.

Each partner will have put up $15,000, plus $5,320 in mortgage amortization costs. A fair estimate of their other costs might be another $1,500 each. Thus, in the first year, each partner will have put up about $22,000 and each partner will have an equity increase of about $9,000—a substantial 41 percent gain. But this does not take into account the tax-deductibility feature of the mortgage payments or any income from the farm. Further, it is not really until the second year that the real payoff begins. In the second year, the farm will be worth $348,100. Each partner's equity will have increased about $25,000. (Remember that the principal sum of the mortgage will be reduced rapidly because of the relatively short payoff period—ten years as compared with the usual thirty-year amount.) Each partner will have paid in about $29,000 and will have already made 86 percent on his money!

(It is well worth noting that the partners' return on their investment is nowhere near as handsome as it would be if the partners had been able to get thirty-year financing with 20 percent down. In that case, their cash outlay would be far smaller and the appreciation would be just as great. Thus the return on cash would be far higher.)

The average farm will double in value in about four years and three months. All that time, each partner will have a $75,000 equity increase and will have paid in about $40,000. It is a fabulous return, but nowhere near as good as if they had the kind of financing homeowners take for granted.

And here comes the balm for the MONEYPOWER reader who has been feeling ill because he could not afford a farm: The very fact of the absence of long-term low-down-payment financing makes farms not much better an inflation hedge than an ordinary house.

The man who buys a $100,000 house with 20 percent down will see almost as good appreciation on his outlay as the man who pays out 30 percent and has to pay off the farm in ten years. It is the low-down-payment, long-term feature that compensates for the more rapid rise in farm prices than house prices.

Look at it with numbers: The man who buys a $100,000 home (by no means a palace in 1979) with 20 percent down, thirty years to pay, will pay $20,000 down and about $650 a month (assuming a mortgage rate of about 9½ percent. In a year he will have paid out about $28,000, not counting the tax-deductibility feature. He will have made $7,000, assuming a 15 percent rise in his house's value. In one year, he will make almost 25 percent on his money. And he will have a place to live! He will double his money in less than three years.

That is not wildly different from the return on the far-faster-rising farm property. It would be tedious (and even frightening) to go into the numbers in detail. Suffice it to say that the lower down payment and long-term payoff features of house financing brings it almost to a par with speculation in farm property, with its far more difficult financing.

To return to the syndication possibility for a moment, it is a useful and profitable venture, but MONEYPOWER cannot recommend it wholeheartedly. A noneconomic factor militates strongly against it. Simply put, it is excruciatingly painful to be involved in any kind of financial venture with people whose own money is at stake. The heartache of dealing with your partners in the syndicate would not allow any joy from the profitability of the venture. Unless the entire process is handled through third parties who are eminently trustworthy and not out to enrich themselves at your expense—and those are hard to find—it is better just to stay away. Life is too short for the pain that partnership brings.

Finally, a warning about farm property. Do not be misled by an agent or by anyone into thinking that the crops raised on the farm will pay any substantial amount of the costs of carrying the property. It simply never happens. The price of farmland is vastly out of proportion to what the farmland produces. No matter how high soybean prices or cattle prices or huckleberry prices go, you will never be able to pay much more than your taxes with the proceeds of the crops.

And so, the definitive MONEYPOWER advice about farms is that if you are rich enough to buy one, do it. Do it with as much borrowed money as possible, that is, or else it is not worth doing. But for the average family, farms have simply passed beyond the stage of affordability. Look and weep as you pass by the contented cows, the waving wheat, and the leafy green fields of money.

PART TWO

Inflation-beating Investments: Golden Traps and Opportunities

7

Golden Opportunities

Imagine a fat man. Day by day he gets fatter. Occasionally he goes on a crash diet and loses a few pounds or holds steady. But only for a few days. Ineluctably, he returns to the table and gets roast pork and sausage and fried eggs and donuts. He gets fatter than ever.

Imagine the fat man's scale. Year by year, as the fat man gains weight, the scale goes higher than before. Occasionally the scale dips or holds steady as the fat man diets, but again, just as sure as sunrise, the reading on the scale goes higher and higher.

Occasionally, well-meaning people and ill-meaning people break into the fat man's bathroom and tamper with his scale so that it reads sharply higher or sharply lower than it would just from registering the fat man's weight. But inevitably the tamperers get bored or get caught, and the scale goes on to register the inexorably greater obesity of the fat man.

The fat man is inflation. The weight on the scale is the price of gold.

Throughout all history, gold has been highly prized. It looks nice as jewelry or ornament. People like to hold it in their hands as coins. Caudillos like to stash it away in Swiss banks. It has industrial uses. People like to put it in their teeth.

And people like to trade their money for it when their money starts to become worthless. And therein lies the allure of gold for the MONEYPOWER strategy. Gold is the very measure of inflation, rising as it rises, just like the fat man's scale rises as he gets fatter. Because gold measures inflation, by definition it goes up in price just as fast as inflation and keeps up with inflation. Think of inflation as a fever and the price of gold as the level of mercury in the thermometer and there you have it.

However, gold is not a precise measurement of inflation. It rises or falls in tandem with and very roughly in the same magnitudes as inflation. It is this imprecision that gives gold added value as an investment medium to triumph over inflation and to let inflation make you rich.

Now if this sounds vague, it can all be cleared up by a little arithmetic and a little history and a little second-order analysis.

There is a finite amount of gold. No government can simply print as much gold as it wants. Even South Africa must strain all its will to produce a small additional amount of gold each year.

There is a potentially infinite amount of money. Governments without principle or discipline can create as much of it as their little hearts desire.

If the only two commodities in the world were gold and printed money, the price for gold would be approximately the number of ounces of gold divided into the number of (let us say) dollars. So, if there were $100 and 100 ounces of gold, there would be a price for gold of $1 for 1 ounce.

Suppose that suddenly some politician created an additional $900 to pay off his supporters. Now there are $1,000. But there are still only 100 ounces of gold. So now the price of gold is $10 per ounce.

This is a simplified, but fundamentally correct, picture of how the price of gold changes and why. The intrinsic value of the gold has not changed. It is simply worth more dollars because there are more dollars and each of the new dollars is worth less. (The example indeed applies to almost any non-money commodity—like housing or farmland—whose supply is relatively fixed.)

Add to the relative increase in gold's cost all the irrational worship of the metal and you get the price explosion of gold in recent years. For gold is a measure of inflation and a way of fleeing inflation as well as an object of dark passions. Gold, properly understood and properly bought, is, after residential single-family houses, certainly the best inflation-riding vehicle there is.

Before we go into the mechanics, let's supplement the arithmetic lesson with a valuable history lesson.

In 1717 Isaac Newton, then a high official of the British Treasury, fixed the price of gold at the sterling equivalent of $20 per ounce. Through all the vicissitudes of the next two centuries, gold stayed at about the same price in Britain and the former colonies. Then, in 1933, hoping to generate some trade during a worldwide depression, Franklin D. Roosevelt devalued the dollar so that 1 ounce of gold was valued at $35.

Although often tottering, gold stayed at that level until 1968, when the United States government stopped pegging the price of gold and allowed it to fluctuate freely in the market.

Five years after that, gold was sold for $100 an ounce. Eighteen months after that, the price of gold on the London market reached $200 on ounce. For about a year after that, gold prices in dollars fell substantially. President Ford imposed a recession on the country to stop inflation (the crash diet in our analogy). And the International Monetary Fund sold off some of its hoard of gold, temporarily flooding the market (the man tampering with the scale in our analogy).

By the summer of 1979, the price of gold had risen to almost $280 an ounce.

It took two centuries for the price of gold to go up by 75 percent.

It took forty years after that for gold to rise in price by 286 percent.

It took five years after that for the price of gold to rise by 280 percent.

You do not need a computer to figure out which way the price is heading and how fast.

Once again, the gold has not changed. It is the same dully gleaming soft metal it always was. The dollars have changed. The price of gold has tracked—though not exactly—the devaluation of the dollar through inflation. Just as land has not changed, gold has not changed. The dollar has changed.

(The accompanying chart illustrates the point exactly. It measures the rise or lack of it in the price of gold denominated in several currencies. The price of gold in dollars, which have inflated dramatically, has risen steeply. The price of gold in Swiss francs, which have hardly depreciated in value at all because of the currency's stability, has hardly changed at all,

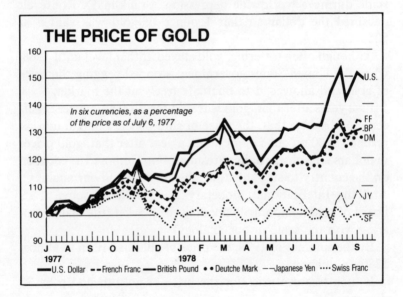

THE PRICE OF GOLD

In six currencies, as a percentage of the price as of July 6, 1977

1977   1978

——U.S. Dollar   – –French Franc   ——British Pound   ● ● Deutche Mark   ——Japanese Yen   ···· Swiss Franc

except in a slight downward direction. Because the Swiss government has refused to allow the franc to inflate, the price of gold in francs actually declined slightly.)

Now we see that the price of gold rises because of inflation in dollars. We see that gold becomes a substitute for dollars right now, in the immediate present. We also see that people buy gold in anticipation of still more inflation. The price of gold reflects not only the inflation that has already occurred, but the amount of inflation that will occur. (Should the anticipation of inflation disappear, the price of gold would fall.) People who buy gold make a bet that the government of the United States will be too uninspired and weak to face up to the problem of inflation and get anything done about it. Gold bugs are betting—not against the United States—but against the people who run the government of the United States.

Considering the number of people who want to bet against the government of the United States and the number who want to bet for the government by buying dollars and selling gold, it is somewhat surprising that gold is not priced higher than it is.

The net of it is that gold is a fine vehicle for getting on top of the crest of inflation waves. But before MONEYPOWER investigates the best ways to invest in gold, it is important that we understand the purposes for which we are interested in gold.

Gold is highly touted not only as an investment medium for relatively normal times, but also as a survival medium. There are many people in this country who believe that we are heading into a period of economic and political turmoil on a truly enormous scale. These people see looming economic depression and anarchy. They see an end to orderly ways of living and trading in America. Blood will flow in the streets, in their scenarios, and simply going down to the bank to cash a check will be as out of the question as going to the moon to cash a check.

For survival, these people believe, the medium of exchange that will be needed is something easily carried, universally appreciated and accepted, and readily stored for the coming emergency. In other words, gold. When the Bolsheviks are running amok, people will still be able to buy the necessities of life with gold. They can still trade the shiny metal for their freedom. And so, these people, who may or may not have a point, like to hold gold.

But their requirements for gold as a survival ration are different from the requirements of the MONEYPOWER investor. The survival ration uses of gold call for easily portable, completely owned small units of gold, so that it can be exchanged for relatively small commodities. The gold must be actually in the physical possession of its owner as well. It does no good for the gold to be held in a bank across the country. Indeed, the survival use of gold dictates that it be held under the mattress or somewhere easily accessible where it can be retrieved in a big hurry.

The MONEYPOWER view of the world is that it will be around, albeit in a steadily deteriorating form, for quite some time yet, and that it is somewhat premature to expect to need gold as a universal medium of exchange for food and shelter. Consequently, the advice that a survival fanatic might consider crucial is not given at all in MONEYPOWER except to note that the preferred ways of using gold to exploit the inflationary situation as set forth here are definitely not the ways that would soothe the brow of a man who fears imminent social collapse.

Now that we have that straight, we can address the four major ways of holding and buying gold.

First, there are gold coins. A few brave countries still mint and circulate coins of almost pure gold. United States citizens are allowed to hold these coins without limitation. These are not antique coins—at least not yet—and their sole value is based upon their gold content.

The three main items in this line are the South African Krugerrand, the Austrian hundred-crown piece, and the Mexican fifty-peso piece.

The price of each coin is usually based on that day's closing price of gold on the London exchange. The Krugerrand contains almost exactly 1 ounce of gold. If gold closed on a certain day at $200 an ounce, a Krugerrand would cost about $200 plus a small premium of a few percent. The same is true for the Austrian and Mexican coins, which contain different amounts of gold. (The Austrian hundred-crown piece is about .98 troy ounces and the Mexican gold peso is 1.2 troy ounces.)

Naturally, as the price of gold rises, the price of these coins rises as well. A Krugerrand bought four years ago would now have doubled in its dollar price at least. The same goes for other coins. The coins are extremely liquid as well. They can be bought and sold at most coin dealers for their gold value less a small commission. For the man who wants to have some of his wealth around him at all times, gold coins are an excellent vehicle.

The careful buyer who plans to buy in quantity will find that it pays to shop around. Some dealers charge slightly more commission or premium than others. Although the difference is trivial on a small purchase, it can mount up.

The main drawback to buying gold coins as an inflation hedge is that there is no leverage to the transaction. To make any money at all doing it, you have to put up an enormous amount of money. For example, if you buy fifty Krugerrands, at prices current as this is written, it will cost about $14,000. If the price of gold goes up by 20 percent, you will make slightly less than 20 percent on your money (because of the commission).

The price of gold will have to more than double before you can double your money. And while that will surely come to pass, it may not come to pass for a long time.

It cannot be denied that the person who bought gold coins

back in 1968 has done well indeed. But the true El Dorado lies farther on.

The second primary way to own gold is to simply buy gold bullion. An ordinary citizen can buy gold bars or lumps of gold bullion, just like the ones in Fort Knox. People can even buy bags of gold dust like the prospectors carried around in the Klondike.

Almost any large broker or commodities dealer can sell you gold bullion. The price is usually about 1 percent above the New York spot price for gold for that day. The size of the minimum purchase varies from dealer to dealer. The most frequent unit of purchase is the "kilobar." As its name implies, a kilobar is 1 kilogram of pure gold. Because a kilogram is about 2.2 pounds, or about 35 ounces, a kilobar today (Summer 1979) might sell for about $9,800.

Some dealers will sell as little as 10 ounces at a time. Usually the buyer leaves the gold with the dealer. The buyer pays a fee for storage and then another fee for assay when the gold is sold.

Commission on this kind of purchase varies, but it is rarely more than 2 percent on each end of the transaction. Prices are usually quoted as "bid" and "asked." The bid price is what buyers are offering, or what you must sell at. The asked price is what you must buy at. The bid price is generally about 2 percent below the asked price.

All of these commissions and spreads between bid and asked mean that when you buy gold bullion, you are immediately down about 3 or 4 percent. That may seem like a tragedy, but it is in fact an extremely modest transactions cost.

A buyer can also buy gold from precious metals companies, which sell gold and silver and perhaps platinum exclusively. Although some of these companies may be respectable, a smart investor stays off back streets. There have been all too many reports of high-pressure sales attempts—sometimes over the telephone. Worse yet, buyers have reported trouble claiming their metal and sellers allege difficulties getting their money when they liquidate their positions. All in all, a fair amount of reticence is in order when dealing with other than a reputable broker in these transactions.

The advantage of buying bullion or dust is just what one might expect: If the price of gold goes up, the price of your holdings of bullion will also go up.

The disadvantage is similar to the disadvantage in buying coins. There is little leverage to the transaction, if any at all. You must put up all of the money to buy the coins and you must put up all of the money to buy the bullion. (In fact, this is not quite true. Some of the less well-known dealers will sell gold bullion and will extend a loan for the purchase. As you hold the gold, you pay out money to service the loan. Unfortunately, this otherwise excellent prospect is flawed. The same companies that sell the gold bullion and make the loans have all too often been accused of bad-faith dealings in the metal, including the withholding of clients' funds.)

If you buy $10,000 worth of gold and the price of gold goes up by 20 percent, you will make about $1,600, after all the commissions. You can see that you must

- Buy a great deal of gold bullion in the first place, or
- Experience a phenomenal increase in the price of gold to truly place yourself well ahead of inflation.

Gold bullion is a conservative, sound hedge against social catastrophe, but it is not exactly suited to the MONEYPOWER strategy of leveraging your way to large profits and financial security on the waves of inflation.

The third primary way to buy gold is to buy gold "futures." Futures are contracts to buy and sell gold at certain prices at certain times in the future.

For example, on Friday, November 10, 1978, an investor could buy a contract to buy 100 troy ounces of gold on January 1, 1979, for $210.10 per ounce. That contract basically repre-

sents a bet that the price of gold will in fact be higher than
$210.10 on January 1, 1979. If it is higher, then the owner
of the contract can sell the contract and make money. If the
actual price of gold on that day is lower than $210.10, the
owner of the contract will lose money.

In the great real world, very few futures contracts are actually ever fulfilled. Hardly any futures traders actually get that
100 ounces of gold delivered to them at the end of the futures
date. As people expect the price of gold to rise and fall, the
price of the contract rises and falls. The contracts themselves
are then sold, rather than the underlying gold.

Again, to take an instance, on November 9, 1978, the world's
gold markets expected the price of gold to fall somewhat in
the near future. Thus, while the price of gold per ounce in a
January 1979 futures contract opened the day at about $217.80
per ounce, the contract closed the day at $210.10 per ounce,
still above the daily spot price, anticipating a rise in the price
of gold. An investor would have lost money on that day's
transaction had he owned a futures contract in January 1979
gold. (In fact, the price soared shortly thereafter, and the buyer
of January 1979 gold would have done well indeed.)

Because each contract is for 100 ounces of gold, the full
price for each contract would be one hundred times the per-
ounce price of gold in the contract. But, in fact, the odds
are quite a lot better than that.

The nature of a futures contract in gold is that it is a predic-
tion that because of inflation the price of gold expressed in
dollars will rise. (Again, remember that the gold has not gotten
more valuable or changed in any way. Dollars have simply
gotten less valuable.) Because of the way futures markets work,
you can make that bet with borrowed money. And *that* is
the way toward significant MONEYPOWER success.

A futures contract in gold is one of many "options" contracts
in the commodities market. For these purposes, gold is considered a commodity like copper or timber. Traditionally, options

contracts can be bought on margin. Usually, an investor can put down as little as about 6 percent to buy a contract in gold. In practice, an investor can buy a contract that covers 100 glittering ounces of gold for $1,250.

Here at last is the kind of MONEYPOWER leverage that we have all been searching for. Before a look at the pitfalls, take a peek at the possibilities. Buying gold on the futures markets is a gamble, but it is just the kind of gamble that MONEYPOWER requires: a bet that the market has not yet anticipated all of the inflation that lies ahead. And that has historically been an excellent bet.

Here is the way it works at its best. (And there can be bad times, too.)

Norman, our MONEYPOWER investor, goes to his broker and opens a margin account in commodities. To do that, he must prove that he has assets of a certain minimum size, as well as give certain legal powers to the broker. Then Norman places on deposit with the broker some minimal sum, such as $5,000, whose purpose, as well as the purposes of the legal entitlements, we shall soon see.

Then Norman tells his broker that he wants to buy a certain contract in gold. On various exchanges, they are offered for delivery at frequent intervals from the immediate future to about three years hence. Let us imagine that he buys February 1980 gold. He is purchasing the chance to buy 100 ounces of gold at $260 on February 1, 1980. (He executed his order on April 2, 1979, early in the morning.) The total contract is worth about $26,000.

For this option, he can pay as little as $1,250 or as much as the full price. Let us imagine, for reasons that will be explained later, that he puts down $3,000.

From then on, he anxiously scans his newspaper for news of the United States government's fumbling of the economic ball, for statistics about growing inflation and decreasing productivity, in the sure and certain knowledge that news of this kind will depress the dollar and elevate the price of gold. He tries not to get alarmed over small movements in either direction, because he does not have the technical or economic expertise to follow the gold market closely enough to be a gold trader on an hourly basis.

Suppose that within a month the price of gold goes up by $15 an ounce—a realistic increase compared to some in recent months. That means the value of his contract will be increased by about $15 times 100 (the number of ounces in his contract). So now his contract is worth about $275 times 100, or $27,500. If Norman now chooses to sell it, he will get a profit of $1,500 less commissions.

The man without second-order analysis might think that Norman has made $1,500 on an investment of $26,000, or 6 percent. That would not be a bad return for one month's time.

But, of course, the investment is far better than that. Norman put up only $3,000 on margin for that transaction. He borrowed the rest from his broker. So his profit was actually $1,500 on $3,000 invested, or very close to *50 percent* in one month.

Now we begin to see why people love options transactions so much. They are about the fastest game in town.

Suppose that Norman believes with all his heart that the inflationary goblin is out of the woods for good, or at least for the next few years. He is confident that although a recession might come along to squeeze down the rate of inflation for a while, we are not going to get out of the inflationary psychology for a long time after the recession has come and gone. Norman holds on to his gold contract for longer than that first month. He holds on while the price of gold goes to $375 an ounce eighteen months after he bought his contract.

Now the original date for delivery of his gold—February 1, 1980—has come and gone. So Norman must trade his contract for one that has a maturity date farther in the future. He decides on an August 1981 contract on the Chicago Mercantile Exchange.

The prices of contracts for delivery far in the future do not correspond penny for penny with the daily price of gold, but the correspondence is close enough so that when gold has gone up $115 an ounce on a spot basis, it will be almost as much higher on an August 1981 contract. (Note well: The prices of gold for delivery far in the future greatly exceed the price for delivery in the near future. For example, on the day in April 1979 when May 1979 gold was selling for $240.10, August 1980 gold was selling for $273. This difference in favor of distant delivery dates is a good measure of just how much inflation and devaluation of the dollar the market expects.)

Suppose that by August 1981 Norman's contract is going for $115 more for every ounce than he paid for it. He will make $11,500 on it when he sells ($115 times 100) less commission. He had, over his eighteen months, made 383 percent on his original $3,000 investment. He has done what we all want to do. He has harnessed the power of inflation to make money with other people's money.

Norman has bet that inflation will continue and that sensible people will continue to flee from the dollar. He has wagered that because of the mystic appeal of gold, it will rise as the dollar falls, but much faster. And he has bet with other people's money, so that if he wins, he will win big.

To be sure, there are no guarantees in life, and there is absolutely no guarantee that Norman will make the kind of money we have been talking about. He could, if he bought more than one contract, make far more. He would simply multiply the gains by the number of contracts. This is how people get rich quick on commodities.

On the other hand, he can lose big too.

If for some reason—and there could be a lot of them—the price of gold drops, Norman has the exact leverage working against him. Suppose that the President orders a drastic increase in the Federal Reserve rediscount rate or announces plans to raise taxes and balance the budget or announces that the federal Treasury will sell off more of our gold supply—then the price of gold might temporarily drop. If it should drop by $15 an ounce, then Norman's February 1980 contract, which he bought at $260 an ounce, would now be worth only $245 an ounce. The total value of the contract would have fallen from $26,000 to $24,500. On his original investment of $3,000, Norman would have lost almost 50 percent.

And even the most avid believer in the inevitability of inflation will concede that there will be occasional times when the price of gold will drop. Sometimes it will drop rapidly.

If the price of gold goes down truly dramatically, Norman or anyone who bought gold on margin could be in a lot of trouble—if he panics.

The danger lies in the "margin" nature of the transaction. Because Norman has bought gold on margin, he has borrowed most of the cost of the contract. The security for the loan is nothing else but the gold. If the price of gold falls by a substantial amount, then obviously the security behind the loan is diminished. If the price falls by enough, the broker will make a "margin call." A margin call is simply a demand for more cash to offset the drop in the value of gold. The broker must be protected on his loan, and if he is not protected by the price of the gold, he will demand protection in increased cash.

That is why Norman had to put up more than the contract price of one gold contract when he began the transaction. Remember that one contract cost $1,250 on minimum margin, but Norman had to put up $5,000 in his account. The extra money is for the broker to lay his hands on quickly if he needs additional margin and the customer is not around.

Remember also that the customer had to sign certain legal documents before he could open his account. They had to do with giving the broker power to charge his account for margin calls.

The legal agreements also had to do with an even more dire possibility, which cannot be foreclosed entirely. If the price of gold drops dramatically and if the customer, our good friend Norman, cannot come up with the additional margin, then the broker can *and will* sell out his contract. The broker will take all the proceeds of the sale to pay off the loan and will bill the client for any deficiency that might be left over. It is a dim possibility, but every MONEYPOWER investor should be aware that over the short term there are sharp fluctuations in the price of gold. The unwary investor can be in for substantial short-term trouble unless he follows certain elementary rules, which MONEYPOWER lays out for him.

First: *Do not panic.* The gold market always fluctuates. No one can reasonably assume that once he buys gold, the whole history of the world will change and from then on the price of gold will go up, up, and away without the slightest downward movement. Fluctuations are to be expected.

Second: Do not simply put down the absolute minimum amount of margin. The less margin you put down, the more likely you are to get a margin call. Margin calls can be profoundly unsettling and are best avoided. If you put down $3,000 instead of $1,250 on margin, you can still have immense leverage. And you will be far less likely to have a margin call.

Third: Look at the next mountaintop and not at the valley. Or, take the long view. The long-term trend of gold is up just as the long-term valuation of the dollar (barring a political epiphany) is down. In between there will be moments when it looks as if the time for holding gold has come and gone. The government will tamper with the gold market or the President will say some high-sounding words about the budget and the price of gold will fall.

That is the temporal equivalent of the valley. There have been a number of them since 1968. But the long-term movement has always been upward, and the peaks after the valleys have always been higher than ever before.

Fourth: Keep your eyes and ears open. The valley could be a long one. If a substantial nationwide tax revolt occurs, if a change of administrations and a change of Congresses occur, then we might see a prolonged period of decline in the price of gold. In that case, the alert MONEYPOWER investor might decide that it is worthwhile to sell out—even at a loss—and buy back in when the recession gets serious and the President announces that the government budget will have to be "temporarily" in deficit. This is an unlikely hypothesis, but it could happen. All inflations do slow down sometime, and this one might, as well. But it will almost surely start back up again. Be prepared.

Fifth: If the whole concept worries the investor too much, which it well could, stay away from it. It is definitely possible, over the short term, to lose more than you have put up on the gold-options market. If that thought keeps you up at night, sell out and forget about it. Speculating in gold options is definitely not for everyone. There is no shame about finding it too nerve-racking.

But if you can take the anxiety and if you have confidence that our national leaders will be mistaken for a good long time, gold-options contracts are a superb way to lay down your bets. They have the weight of history behind them. They are highly liquid. And they let you make money with other people's money. They are the second-best MONEYPOWER investment, after residential dwellings.

The fourth major way to hold gold is to buy stock in gold-mining companies. Simple as it may sound, gold-mining companies mine gold. Then they sell it. If the price of gold is high, the companies make money. If the price is low, the companies make less money.

There are gold-mining companies in the United States, Canada, and the Union of South Africa. Their shares are traded on various exchanges including the New York Stock Exchange, the American Stock Exchange, and the over-the-counter market. Some of them are long-established companies that have been pulling ore out of the ground for decades. Others have

just been formed and it is unclear just what they are mining—
the ground or the public's insatiable gullibility about gold.

Gold-mining-company shares are an excellently leveraged
way of holding gold in a way completely different from the
way options contracts are leveraged.

The leverage works in two ways. First, imagine that the
Mother Lode Mining Company has one large share of stock.
That stock controls all of the company and receives all the
earnings. The Mother Lode company can mine all the gold
it wants at a cost of mining of $150 per ounce. If the cost of
gold on the open market is $125 an ounce, the company is
in trouble. If the price is $150 an ounce, the Mother Lode
company is breaking even, just about. If the price is $175 an
ounce, the company is making money, which goes to that
one big share.

Now if the price of gold goes up to $200 an ounce, the
Mother Lode company will double its earnings per ounce of
gold even though the price of gold has risen by only 14 percent.
If the price goes to $225 an ounce, the earnings per ounce
will triple, even though the price of gold has risen by only
28 percent.

Because there is only one share of the Mother Lode company,
all earnings immediately accrue to that share. Its price will
be a multiple of earnings—say six—times the multiple that
the earnings per ounce of gold has gone up. There is real
leverage.

For example, if the stock was selling at $10 per share, it
might well go to $30 if the price of gold rose by as little as
28 percent. These are the kinds of gains, in a smooth situation,
that one might expect from rising gold prices.

The second kind of leverage that gold-mining-company
shares have is based on their corporate debt.

If the Mother Lode Mining Company has total capital of
$1 million of which $100,000 is stock and the rest is bonds
paying 8 percent, it can achieve some remarkable leverage.

If it earns 10 percent overall on its capital, that represents the sum of $100,000. Most of that, some $72,000, will be needed to pay off the interest on the debt. The rest, $28,000, can be applied to the equity. That means the equity is paying 28 percent, not bad by any standard.

The principle of this kind of leverage is exactly the same as MONEYPOWER explained for the homeowner. The Mother Lode company—like the homeowner—is earning money not only on its own money (the stock), but on the bondholders' money, and all of that surplus (on the bondholders' money) goes to the stock.

Compound those two kinds of leverage together and truly awesome leverage can be created.

In theory then, the gold-mining companies should stand to profit richly from increases in the price of gold. They have the leverage, both internal and external, to multiply gold price rises handsomely. The only alteration from the example is that there is not one share, but many shares, and the profits can be spread over them.

And, indeed, gold-mining stocks have done well during the recent inflation. In the period since 1968, when the Dow-Jones Industrials as a group did not come anywhere near keeping up with inflation, the index of gold-stock prices more than doubled the rate of inflation.

In addition, gold-mining-company stocks listed on the major exchanges and the over-the-counter market are extremely liquid, with low transaction costs.

Still, there are problems with gold-mining stocks. The main problem is that when you buy a kilobar of gold, you know just how much gold you are getting. When you buy stock in a gold mine, you do not by any means know how much gold you are getting. There may be years of good digging left at that mine or there may be nothing there after a few months. Moreover, it is not always in the interests of the management of the gold-mining company to tell their investors just how much gold is really down there—even if they know.

Second, the purchase of gold-mining stocks involves the exact same problems that purchasing any stocks involves. The stock buyer is completely at the mercy of the management. When a clever investor buys gold, he knows what he is getting. Gold. When an investor buys stock in a gold-mining company, he gets a company, with all the problems of a company, and also some gold. If the management is inefficient in getting that gold out, the stockholder pays for it. If the management of the company is using company funds to pay for the new Jacuzzi of the board chairman's girl friend, the stockholder pays for it.

(In all fairness, these views about stock corporations are not conventional views. Many people take for granted that the management of any significant stock company will run it in a legitimate and aboveboard way. Many people assume that the management of a stock company will run it in the interests of the shareholders instead of the interests of the management. Others wish they could believe that.)

On the plus side again, holding stock in gold-mining companies is one of the only ways—perhaps the only way—to take a flyer on gold and also earn dividends. For years, one of the main objections to holding gold was that it paid no interest, royalties, or dividends. Those objections were heard far more before the price of gold began to shoot into the stratosphere, but still they are heard. Certain gold-mining stocks pay an excellent dividend, thus contradicting the notion that there is no income from holding gold except capital-gains income.

In particular, gold-mining companies in South Africa pay good dividends, largely to compensate for investor concern about South Africa's political situation. Some North American gold shares pay in the neighborhood of 10 percent, even with current high prices.

In principle, gold-mining shares are an excellent application of the MONEYPOWER strategy. They allow an investor to benefit from the inflationary surge in gold prices that is likely to be with us for some time. Moreover, their prices are raised by leverage on both earnings and debt-equity ratios.

If the MONEYPOWER investor can find a gold-mining company in whose management he reposes special trust, he will have an extremely good vehicle for capitalizing on inflation. But to buy any gold-mining company that comes down the pike is simply giving money to strangers. MONEYPOWER requires a careful look at the company, its prospects as rated by independent experts, and some knowledge of the management.

Once satisfied on those counts, a MONEYPOWER investment in gold-mining stocks can be a fine way to gain substantial power against inflation. Do not look for the enormous gains that can be yours in the options market when things go your way; be content with the quite respectable advances that can and will make the right gold-mining stock a joy to own, without the roller-coaster anxieties that beset some options investors.

To sum up the MONEYPOWER view of gold:

For the survival-minded, gold coins and gold bullion are excellent for peace of mind.

For the investor with nerves of steel, the true believers in their destiny of growing rich through inflation, contracts in the gold-options market can hardly be beat.

For the more hesitant investor who likes leverage but is willing to let someone else actually count the money, and who does not mind doing a lot of research before he puts down his money, gold-mining stocks can be just the ticket.

The main thing to remember in terms of gold is that it is the measure of inflation. If inflation continues hot—and there is every sign that it will—gold will continue upward feverishly. When there are signs that inflation is cooling, gold will drop. In the long run, while that man keeps getting fatter—while everyone thinks inflation will trend upward—gold will rise like the weight on the scale. MONEYPOWER tells us that it has already eased the inflation fears of hundreds of thousands, and it can do exactly the same for any careful investor.

8

The Gnomes of
Main Street

Remember the gnomes of Zurich? They were the currency speculators in Zurich who relentlessly drove down the value of the British pound about ten years ago. Harold Wilson, Labor Prime Minister of Britain, explained that the reason the pound kept falling in foreign-exchange markets had nothing to do with the intrinsic value of the pound. It was all the dirty dealings of the gnomes of Zurich, he said. Nevertheless, the pound kept falling. That is, it kept falling until two things happened:

First, the British found that there was a great deal of oil off the coast of Scotland.

Second, the British put the screws on inflation, bringing it down drastically from the 25 to 30 percent rate that had sent the pound plummeting.

While all this was going on, the gnomes of Zurich were making a great deal of money. Men on the street envied the wheeler-dealers who manipulated currencies to make themselves rich. Here were men who held in their hot little hands the precious stuff we use to pay our bills. Those gnomes transferred millions of pounds' worth all over the world to make money trading in the stuff we consider sacred relics. To them, money was just another commodity like pork bellies or cotton. That is just how brave and above it all the currency speculators look to us peons down below.

Now for the secret. There is no rite of initiation, no blood bond, no sinful oath that makes a person a currency speculator. Anyone with a minimum of $5,000 can become a currency speculator. And maybe you should become one. It is a risky and dangerous game, but it can pay off dramatically in the age of inflation.

Here is why it pays off so handsomely, or at least why it often pays off so handsomely. Suppose that the world is a neighborhood populated by children playing with marbles. One child is America and one is Germany and one is Japan and one is Switzerland. Each child begins the day's trading with the same number of marbles of the same size. One day, the child named America appears with twice as many marbles, each half the size of the other children's marbles. When the moment comes to exchange marbles, the other kids will demand that they get more of those smaller marbles for each of their larger marbles. So the rate of exchange between American marbles and Japanese marbles will be about two American marbles to one Japanese marble.

Then suppose that on the very next day, the child named America shows up with even smaller marbles, and even more of them, and he will not let the other children have any of the older, larger marbles any longer. Naturally, the children will demand that they get still more of the smaller American marbles per each of their larger marbles. Gradually, the other children will be loaded with small American marbles and they will barely even consider taking any more of those little American marbles unless the exchange rate allows them a great many of those pitiful American marbles for their wholesome large marbles.

That is basically what has happened to the American currency. As the dollar has been devalued for inflation, each American dollar becomes like a smaller, more nearly worthless marble. After all, what can be bought with each of the dollars is steadily less.

Because certain of the other countries in the world, notably Germany, Japan, and Switzerland (and to a lesser extent, Britain), refused to inflate and devalue their currencies, they have had the equivalent of the big, wholesome marbles.

Thus, when we read the almost daily declines in the dollar that accompany our inflationary cycles, we are witnessing the exact analogue of the story of the marbles. Our dollars are becoming steadily smaller and other countries demand steadily more of them in exchange for their currencies.

A cautionary note. Imagine that the American child's mother complains to the other children's mothers that because of the way the other children are trading, she will pull her child out of the game—or maybe beat them up—unless they pay him a little more for his marbles. She also promises that in the future, she will refuse to let her baby make his marbles so small.

That is the exact equivalent of what the American government occasionally does in the foreign-exchange markets. Citing the threat to world trade and order, the United States forces the countries with stable prices—Japan, Germany, Switzerland—to use their valuable money to prop up the sagging American money. The aid from the stable-currency countries is always accompanied by promises from the United States that it will stop inflating and will stabilize its currency.

Now, in fact, these emergency actions by other countries to rescue the Yankee dollar rarely work. They are like a bankrupt man borrowing still more money from unwary creditors so that he can give a lavish dinner. The dinner is supposed to persuade people that he is not really broke. In fact, after the dinner he is more broke than ever, and the creditors all eventually realize it.

And if all of these metaphors and explanations are too confusing, one need only remember the basic economic fact of life of currency trading. When country A is experiencing faster inflation than other countries, country A's currency will generally be worth less in terms of the other countries' currencies.

Now to the mechanics. How does an ordinary citizen transform himself into a gnome of Zurich, speculating and prospering on the inflationary excesses of his country's elected and appointed leaders?

The basic process is similar to that necessary to open an account at a brokerage to trade in gold-options contracts. Typically, the customer, Norman, goes to a broker and establishes that he has a certain minimum net worth and income qualifications. He then deposits a sum of money, usually in the vicinity of $5,000, and opens an account. He must also sign certain legal documents.

He can then buy and sell contracts for delivery of foreign currencies. These contracts are similar indeed to contracts for future delivery of any commodity, including gold. The contracts specify that on a certain day the holder of the contract may purchase a certain quantity of foreign currency at a certain price. For example, in Spring 1979, Norman could have bought a contract for delivery of 125,000 Swiss francs on September 1, 1979, at a price of 61.54 cents per Swiss franc.

That means that on September 1, 1979, no matter what the spot, or current, price of the Swiss franc might be, Norman can buy 125,000 of them for 61.54 cents each. Let us imagine that the dollar has continued to decline in value and the Swiss franc has held relatively steady in value. Then the Swiss franc might have gone up perhaps 5 percent in value above the contract price. On March 1, 1979, it might be quoted at 64.59 cents.

Now bear in mind that we are dealing with a large number of Swiss francs. If the contract price per Swiss franc is multiplied by the contract quantity, we find that the original contract cost was worth $76,987.50. After the continued appreciation of the Swiss franc to 64.59 cents each, the contract could be sold for $80,738.00. The profit is $3,751.00.

Of course, as with all futures contracts, the contract is hardly ever actually delivered. As the daily prices of currencies change and as inflationary expectations change, the contract prices change. Norman will in all likelihood liquidate his contract long before the date for delivery of his Swiss francs. The contract price will have given him his profit (or loss), depending upon the expectations of what the price *would have been* on the day of delivery had delivery actually taken place.

In our example, Norman has made a profit of about $4,000. That may not seem like a lot on a total capital sum of over $80,000. But, in fact, Norman can and should buy his currency on margin. Just as people buy other commodity futures on margin, they can also buy futures contracts in foreign currencies on margin.

Margin requirements change from month to month during periods of hectic trading, but at the present moment (fall 1978), they are about $2,500 to open a contract. That means that the relatively tiny sum of $2,500 controls almost $80,000 worth of Swiss francs. There is leverage indeed.

More to the point, if Norman has bought his Swiss-franc contract with the minimum margin, he has put down only about 3 percent margin! A 5 percent gain in the price of the currency means an incredible approximate doubling of the speculator's money.

All of this means that the power to make money—with other people's money—because of inflation is greater with currency speculation than with any other medium in general use.

Imagine that a 1 percent rise in the value of Swiss francs against the dollar generates an incredible 33 percent rise in the contract's value when the contract is bought on the minimum margin. Again, this can happen because the investor is able to control a vast amount of currency with an extremely small margin.

Margins and leverages in other currencies are almost equivalently astonishing. For $2,500, an investor can buy a contract for 12.5 million yen. At recent rates of exchange (about 210 yen to the dollar), such a contract was worth about $60,000. If the yen appreciates by 1 percent, again the profits are extraordinary.

Again, the difference in price, tiny though it is on a per yen basis, is magnified enormously by the huge number of yen in the contract and the enormous leverage in the margin feature.

How much can be made if there is a truly enormous inflation in American currency relative to foreign currency? Well, in 1973 each yen was worth about .34 cents. In the Spring of 1979 each yen was worth about .47 cents. That is a .38 percent rise in the value of the yen against the dollar.

If Norman had a contract for 12.5 million yen in 1974, it would have been worth $42,500. The same contract, had he kept renewing it (at some frictional cost), would now be worth $58,750. On an investment of $2,000 (which was the cost of opening a margin account in yen in 1974), Norman would have made a $17,000 profit, or over 900 percent.

The fact is that when inflation starts to move a currency in the direction that the MONEYPOWER investor wants it to go, the leverage is simply phenomenal. Small wonder that the gnomes of Zurich get rich quick. (Or poor quick. We will get to that directly.)

The leverage in contracts in Deutsche marks is just as good. A margin requirement of $2,000 will control a contract for 125,000 marks. In the Spring of 1979 each mark was worth about 55 cents. That means each 125,000-mark contract was worth about $66,250. Or in other words, the investor is putting up about 3 percent margin.

(On the yen speculation the margin rate is almost exactly the same and not by coincidence.)

There are similarly low margins and correspondingly huge leverages in speculation in Canadian dollars (not a good bet because they are inflating even faster than the United States) and British pounds.

It is important to realize that no one is going to actually sell the investor that huge amount of foreign currency for those few margin dollars. The investor is buying a contract for future delivery of foreign currency and not actual wads of money.

But for all practical purposes—except running off to Rio with the money—the transaction is the same. The investor is making an immense bet on the currency markets with borrowed money.

Key question: Is the trend of recent history running in favor of speculating against the dollar and for foreign currencies in which there is a market?

Take a look.

In 1965 the Swiss franc was worth 23.11 cents. In 1970 the Swiss franc was worth 23.20 cents. Not exactly a major change. By 1973, the Swiss franc was up to 31.70 cents. By 1975 the Swiss franc was up to 38.74 cents, and in the Spring of 1979 it is about 59 cents. In other words, the Swiss franc took five years to go up by less than 1 percent (1965–70), three years go up 55 percent (1970–73), and five years after that to go up 71 percent!

In 1965 the Deutsche mark was worth 25.04 cents. In 1970 it was worth 27.42 cents, an increase of barely more than 8 percent in five years. But by 1973 the Deutsche mark was worth 37.76 cents, an increase of almost 38 percent in three years. And now, in Summer 1979, the DM is about 54 cents, another 43 percent increase since 1973.

The rise of the yen is the most spectacular of all. To short-cut all of the boring statistical year-to-year comparisons, MONEYPOWER notes simply that the yen has moved from .28

cents in 1970 (a level it had been stuck at for years) to about
.47 cents in Spring 1979. That marks a 68 percent increase
in only eight years.

Currency speculation against the dollar and in favor of stable
foreign currencies is obviously a superb MONEYPOWER investment in many ways.

- It allows the investor to make money with borrowed money
- It embodies movement in the same direction as inflation but
  much faster
- It is completely liquid

In other words, it uses the forces of inflation and borrowing
to allow an investor to make money with it much faster than
he loses money because of inflation.

But there are red warning flags posted all over currency
speculation that need explaining.

For one thing, currency speculation is only for the bravest,
coolest hands around town. Just as price changes in your favor
can make you rich overnight, price changes against you can
hurt badly. For example, if Norman, our MONEYPOWER investor, puts down 3 percent margin on yen and the yen declines
against the dollar by 1 percent he will get a margin call immediately. If the yen goes down by as little as 3 percent, Norman
would lose his investment totally.

And if, by some catastrophe, the yen depreciated against
the dollar by as much as 10 percent, Norman would be in
the hole for margin calls three times as large as his original
investment.

The leverage that works in the MONEYPOWER investor's
favor so mightily can also work against him. Now it is important to realize that the trends of history are certainly running
in favor of those who bet that the dollar will depreciate as
against the currencies of our major free-world economic partners.

But there are eddies and riptides in the overall currents of man's affairs. For example, if the United States begins to go into a recession at just about the time Japan goes into a major boom, we will see serious—albeit temporary—movements against the currents of the postwar period. Similarly, if Japan's price level rises faster than America's, the yen will fall.

Typically, a country in a recession sees its currency appreciate against the currencies of countries undergoing boom times. The reason is simply the relative levels of demands for exports and imports of countries in recession and countries in boom. Although the United States already has so many dollars floating around the world that the effects of a short recession would probably be small, nevertheless the effects might be enough to seriously discomfit the MONEYPOWER investor who either cannot afford to wait for a change in movements or is too upset to wait for such a movement in his favor. Remember— do not speculate against the dollar when the United States is going into a recession or if foreign inflation is greater than American.

Moreover, even independent of recessions and booms, there are serious day-to-day changes in currency prices that can lay low all but the most toughened speculator. A word from a Prime Minister here and a hint from a Secretary of the Treasury there, and all of a sudden, sensible trends are upset— even if only for a few days.

The basic problem with currency speculation as opposed to gold speculation is that there are two variables in currency speculation—the dollar and the other currency. In gold speculation there is only one variable—the value of the dollar. The gold stays exactly the same from century to century. (Although even here, there can be tampering. The International Monetary Fund can sell gold or the U.S. Treasury can sell gold or there can be riots in Soweto. But these are less uncertain and treacherous. Basically gold is gold.)

But if the MONEYPOWER investor takes a few precautions similar to the precautions in gold, he can save himself some of the heartache that can go with unsuccessful currency trading.

First, it is foolhardy to put down the absolute minimum amount of margin. If the MONEYPOWER investor puts down 5 or 6 percent instead of 3 percent margin, he is in a far better position to weather the inflationary or deflationary crosscurrents that affect the currency market. He will not be subject to those upsetting early-morning margin calls that can ruin an otherwise perfect day.

Second, if everyone is predicting that the United States is about to go into a recession or that Japan will have a major inflation, he should stay out of the foreign-exchange market on the buying side. All the experts might be wrong, but why should he take a chance and fly in the face of the expert opinion?

Third, if the exchange markets are highly roiled and thin, and if each day brings a dramatic change in the price of dollars or yen, stay away. If the investor is hep enough and well wired enough to profit from fishing in those shark-infested waters, he does not need advice. If the game is being played by barracudas, that is the time to sit it out.

When quieter times have returned, then a flyer in foreign currency might be well worthwhile. Look for the days when inflation is roaring along but the country has just recently come out of a recession. That way, no one will be suggesting that we should go back into a recession any time soon.

Look for the usual signs of heightened inflation here at home—a large government deficit, promises of easier money by the Federal Reserve Board, demands for more social-welfare spending by militant special interests, constantly falling productivity. Those are the signposts that lead the alert MONEYPOWER investor to the time and the place for currency speculation.

Even with all the precautions, currency speculation is not for the young couple just starting out with barely enough money to get by. Nor is it for the hard-pressed wage earner saving for his daughter's orthodontia and his son's college. Again, it is not for the older man or woman living on a fixed income and with limited resources.

You can win very big in foreign-currency speculation. Buying options on the currency of Germany, Japan, or Switzerland has been perhaps the very best inflation hedge in the postwar period. It has paid profits vastly, stupendously greater than the rate of inflation. For the man with some extra money, which he can invest and not lose sleep over if he loses it, foreign-currency speculation can be perfect.

But the investor, even the alert investor, can lose big and lose fast in currency trading. It is for those who can afford to lose and not for any others.

9

Cautions and Warnings

The three investment vehicles described so far in MONEY-POWER strategy are far from conventional vehicles. Single-family houses, gold futures, and currency options, although by far the most loaded in favor of *beating* inflation, are nevertheless somewhat off the beaten path. This means that they must be tailored to the needs of the individual. The strategies are not equivalently suited to everyone in every situation. So here are some guidelines. If they are strict, they are strictly designed to keep the MONEYPOWER investor from going astray.

The housing vehicle is by far the least risky. It is best suited for the individual or family who has not yet begun to accumulate the capital that can keep them from privation. With an adequate degree of care in selecting the neighborhood, a purchase of a house can hardly go wrong during this inflationary epoch. It requires only a small down payment, and it allows for the accumulation of equity while paying for a service—housing—that would have to be paid for anyway.

Young couples or middle-aged people without significant resources might begin their anti-inflation MONEYPOWER strategy with real property. It is also an ideal situation for a couple approaching retirement who want to be certain to build up the largest possible estate. (Beware, however, of undertaking large debt service at a time when your income will be declining. Nothing can be worse in an inflationary era than paying off plentiful debts with scarce dollars. If you are about to retire, be *sure* that the mortgage-service payments will be within your means even when your income is reduced *and* even if the other items in your budget will rise rapidly—as they assuredly will.)

The real-estate investment in which stages two and beyond are entered—namely taking the equity out of prior homes to buy rental property—is also ideally suited to the family with one wage earner and one spouse who has some free time. Inevitably, some amount of aggravation and attention will be required to maintain rental properties. This is neither more nor less than the nature of human life. The single man or woman who cannot take time from work to see that the electrician arrives will find himself or herself seriously hindered in managing the property in question. No property manager is likely to be an adequate substitute for one's own examination of the pros and cons of any renovation or repair.

The gold investment is for the man or woman who already has some real estate and who can afford to take a flyer on an investment that is a good bet in the long run but can be treacherous in the short run. It is definitely not a substitute for buying a house or even two or three houses. Gold should be entered into as a speculation only when an investor has a home and enough financial security to afford the valleys that may come before the mountains.

Arbitraging from currency into gold and back into currency is historically a superb method for beating inflation. It has been since the days of ancient Athens. But it has also been an investment for the stout of heart and the firm of mind. Under no circumstances should anyone put his last dollar into speculating on gold. Once the MONEYPOWER investor is one up above what he needs realistically for the foreseeable future, then he can start thinking about gold.

Gold options are a particularly good MONEYPOWER vehicle

for the older man or woman who has some money and wants to assure that it is not run into nothing by inflation. Such a person has the time to study economic conditions closely and watch for the economic signs that tell whether it is time to buy or sell.

Under no circumstances should anyone who takes a position in gold go anywhere incommunicado and leave his or her gold positions uncovered. The annals of finance are littered with the corpses (figuratively speaking) of those who came back from that charming little out island in the Bahamas and found that they were sold out because of margin calls they could not be reached to make. Worse yet are the tales of people who left no instructions about when to sell. Too often they came back to find that the market had become so chaotic that they could not be sold out at any price near break-even. And so when they finally could be sold out, the sale was at a sadly low price. Bear it in mind—a gold investment needs careful watching. The investor needs to learn about daily limits and margin calls.

But, if the investor is careful and well prepared, options in gold can take him from worry about inflation far into the stratosphere of financial security for life. If the investor has the will to learn and the courage to face a tricky short-term market, over the long term, he can make himself rich. In real dollars.

Most tricky of all, and most rewarding of all, are the currency markets. They are leveraged so spectacularly that even a small movement in your direction can take all the worry out of retirement. But they can go against the investor in the short run just as gold can. MONEYPOWER requires following the rules of good sense about when to get on that particular merry-go-round and when to get off.

The man or woman who goes in for currency trading must

be able to follow economic news and currency-market trading closely. He or she must also never put up more than he or she can afford to see wiped out in a week of furious trading. Yes, when the profits start to come in, liquidate and use your profits to acquire still more options. That way lies the safest possible way to making out like a bandit. No pensioners on their uppers, no young couples just starting out should even dream of plunking down their nickels on currency trading.

But, for the man or woman with a large net worth—or a significant one at least—who sees his or her wealth evaporating under the sweltering sun of inflation, currency trading can be manna from heaven. More important than adequate assets and serenity, however, is the fact that the currency trader must stay on top of the market all the time. It is a full-time job, but one that pays very well.

And crucially, in all of these investments, bear in mind the life or death importance of the sleeping point. That is the point at which you become so worried about investments that you can barely sleep. Once you reach that point—back off. It is far better to see your money gradually worn away by inflation than to see yourself growing more haggard daily with worry over your investments.

No investment yet devised is worth one instant in the intensive-care unit.

A final note on gold and currency trading. Is that speculation against the dollar the same as speculating against America? Is it unpatriotic or morally wrong?

Moral and patriotic judgments can rarely be made in the absolute, but MONEYPOWER believes that speculating in gold or currency is not only far from unpatriotic, but is a positive help to this country.

The true situation is this: Politicians obsessed with buying votes have systematically robbed the people of America of their savings and their security by devaluing the currency.

The crew in Washington has over the last ten years simply taken 50 percent of the value of the dollar here at home (far more abroad) to pay for their vanities.

By buying gold or foreign currencies, the MONEYPOWER investor is doing no more than signaling his or her disgust with the way the money of this country has been plundered by politicians. The MONEYPOWER investor is moreover trying to save himself or herself from a man-made disaster comparable—in the loss of purchasing power of money—with the loss of productivity in the Great Depression of 1929–39. What should it be called when a lawless mob takes the reins of power and tries to steal money from the citizens? And what should it be called when the citizens attempt to save themselves without violence?

When the men in power attempt to deplete the national treasure, it can hardly be called a patriotic act. By the same token, when the ordinary citizen attempts to save his own treasure within the law and by peaceful means, that hardly seems unpatriotic.

The ultimate result of speculation against the dollar is to create a climate of falling dollar values and falling confidence in the men who run this country. That, on occasion, can make those men act decently at least for a brief while.

Still, there will undoubtedly be those who think it is unpatriotic to speculate against the dollar. That is part of human nature. But when the government starts to proclaim that currency speculation by American citizens is wrong—watch out. Dictatorial governments without sound policies have always, always *always* blamed their own failures on currency speculators.

When the Jacobins erected their tumbrels in the Place de la Concorde, the first places were reserved for those who correctly saw the chaos that revolutionary terror would bring to France and sought to speculate on it. When Lenin plunged Russia into confusion, the ordinary citizen could see immediately that there were fewer rather than more of the necessities of life. Lenin blamed it on currency speculators. The same has been true in Hitler's Germany and Mao's China.

A government that cannot understand economics and cannot bring decent standards of living to its people will always blame its own failure on currency (and gold) speculators.

When a President appears on prime-time television and explains that the nation's problems are the fault of the currency speculators, it is time to beware. Such complaints are an admission of utter failure in promulgating responsible economic policy. Far more seriously, they are a trumpet flourish announcing a threat to freedom. The end of freedom for people to speculate with their money as they please is almost inevitably the beginning of the end of far broader freedoms.

For now, the freedom to save oneself through speculation in gold and currency exists. For the right people it is an opportunity that should not be overlooked. There is no telling how long it will last.

10

Posted: Keep Out

Some numbers to conjure with:

The monthly average Dow-Jones Industrial Average for 1965 was 910.

The monthly average Dow-Jones Industrial Average for 1970 was 753.

For 1971 it was 884.

For 1972 it was 950.

For 1973 it was 923.

For 1975 it was 803.

On April 2, 1979 it was 855.

More numbers to conjure with: the monthly average of the New York Stock Exchange common-stock index, a far more broadly based measurement than the Dow:

1965	47.39
1970	45.72
1971	54.22
1972	60.29
1973	57.42
1974	43.84
1975	45.73
April 2, 1979	56.73

The point could be made with the NASDAQ Index, Standard & Poor's, the American Stock Exchange Index, or any

110

other reputable index. Common stocks, preferred stocks, over-the-counter stocks, all stocks point in the same direction. Stocks are simply not a good inflation hedge. Unless the alert investor has inside information of an absolutely ironclad nature (and acting on this sort of information is generally illegal), guaranteed in blood to make the stock go up, he might just as well stay away from stocks.

Bear in mind that the indexes above are indexes of prices *in current dollars*. That means the indexes simply tell what the averages of certain prices are on a given day. In other words, there is no adjustment for inflation in those prices. Usually, a price unadjusted for inflation is startlingly higher in 1978 than in 1965. After all, the Consumer Price Index has risen over 100 percent since 1967. But the leading indexes of stock prices simply have not even kept up with inflation, let alone kept ahead of it.

In other words, unless you have a special situation—a real one, where your wife's sister is married to the board chairman, not a false one, where your stockbroker says his research department knows something that everybody else at Harry's American Bar knows—stay away from the stock market.

At one time common stocks on the New York or American stock exchanges were an excellent inflation hedge. In the period from the end of World War II to the mid-1960s, the prices of stocks on the New York Stock Exchange grew far more rapidly than inflation. Whereas the Consumer Price Index rose by about 45 percent from V-J Day to 1965, the Dow-Jones Industrial Average rose by almost 1,000 percent.

That stupendous rise in the postwar period is still throwing off the statistics on just how good an inflation-beating vehicle stocks really are. If the measurement includes the entire postwar period, the price rise in the Dow still looks excellent, even compared with the rate of inflation.

But the real question is just how good common stocks (or preferred stocks) have done against inflation since 1965, when the forces of inflation started to rise full steam ahead. And by those standards, the picture is gloomy indeed. To put it succinctly, stock prices have been in a hidden depression since the Vietnam War. The only reason the magnitude of the disaster is not apparent is that inflation has kept prices from readily showing their true levels. If the proper adjustments were made for inflation, the Dow would be less than 400 in fall 1978.

MONEYPOWER strategy does not pretend to know all the reasons why the stock market has done so poorly in relation to inflation. Certainly part of the reason is inflation itself. As capital stock wears out, the allowance for depreciation, which the company has taken, is no longer nearly adequate to cover the replacement cost of new capital. Therefore the companies must either forgo new capital or take the money for capital out of profits. Either way, the company is a less powerful profit-making force.

Taxes make no allowance for inflation, constantly eating away funds needed to replace aging equipment.

Government imposes horrendous new costs upon business for complying with regulations on safety and environmental protection without making any allowance for spreading those costs onto the true beneficiaries.

Workers' productivity constantly falls as the work force becomes less motivated and disciplined.

And finally, investors lose faith in the entire free-enterprise system.

That is where the stock market is today. Investors simply place a low value on the future profits of business corporations, and therefore the stock market stays low. Stock prices are after all only estimates of the flow of future earnings from the issuing company.

The net of it all is that the MONEYPOWER strategy recommends strongly against investment in stocks unless the investor has clearly valuable inside information about the stock's likely future earnings. And, once again, it is generally illegal to act upon such information anyway.

Someday there may be a breakthrough in scientific know-how that will not be hamstrung by the environmentalist Luddites. Someday there may be a generation of workers who want to work. Someday there may be an administration that does not kill the geese that lay the golden eggs. And someday the stock market may once again be a lively instrument for defeating inflation. But not now.

The same melancholy conclusion leaps out at the MONEY-POWER investor whenever the bond market comes up. Bonds are not quite as desperately poor an investment as stocks because of the high interest they now pay. But still, the history is depressing.

In 1950 Standard & Poor's Municipal Bond Index stood at 133.4. It has declined almost monotonically since then until by the fall of 1978 it stood at 55.

There has been an even steeper decline in the selling price of the U.S. government long-term bonds index and the corporate AAA-rated securities.

As everyone knows, bond prices move in the opposite direction to bond interest rates. That means that in the last decade, as new bond yields have skyrocketed—so that bond sellers can raise money in the era of permanent inflation—the average yield of all bonds has had to keep pace. That means—of necessity—that bond prices must fall to equalize the return.

(To understand the phenomenon, imagine that all bonds were issued for perpetuity, so that they never matured. Their price would then be solely a function of their return.

(Bond A was issued in 1950, paying the then current yield of 2.5 percent, if you can believe it. It was priced at $1,000 and had a coupon of $25 a year.

(Time passes and now, in 1979, bonds will yield about 9½ percent. That means that a bond with $1,000 face value will have a coupon of $95.

(No one on earth will hold that corporation Bond A at face value. They will sell it until its price falls to $263, at which point the $25 coupon will represent a yield of 9½ percent. This is exactly why the average price of bonds consistently falls. They must fall so that investors will realize the same yield from them as from other, newer debt.)

Because there is no prospect for anything but higher interest rates, there is little prospect of capital appreciation in bonds. Bond prices only rise, after all, when yields fall.

Bond yields are definitely high during this inflationary episode. Often they exceed the current rate of inflation, which is true for few other interest-bearing instruments. Especially if an investor goes in for slightly below AAA bonds, yields can be above 10 percent. In historical terms, 10 percent or higher seems like an excellent yield.

In fact, it is not. One hectic week of money-supply tightening can raise the interest rate for all bonds by a full point. Suddenly the yield does not look quite as good. Moreover, to sell the bond and buy another instrument yielding better interest would require selling at a level painfully lower than the price at which the investor bought in. So in a period of rising interest rates, the investor loses money not only on the yield of his bond but also on the price of the bond.

The sad fact is that in an era of incessantly rising interest rates—which is what an inflationary era is—the ownership of instruments of long-term indebtedness is a mistake. Such ownership—of a bond, for example—is a bet that interest rates have peaked and that the bond you own will turn out to have a higher yield at the time of purchase than subsequent yields. For those who believe such a bet is sensible, MONEYPOWER offers the following helpful numbers.

In 1950 the average yield on the forty bonds in Moody's Industrials was 2.67 percent.

In 1955, the same statistic was 3.19 percent.

In 1960 the yield was 4.59 percent.

In 1965 the yield was 4.61 percent.

In 1970 the yield was 8.26 percent.

In 1975 the yield was 9.26 percent.

As of early 1979 the yield was just over 10 percent.

Certainly, as money-market conditions tighten and ease, yields change. A yield may actually fall for a period of months as an average number because of money-supply conditions. But the long-term trend is definitely upward for yields. By the same token, the long-term prospects for bondholders are unsatisfactory under the MONEYPOWER strategy.

Even municipal bonds with the feature of escaping federal tax on the coupon are a fraud as an inflation-beating device.

First, the tax-free feature is meaningless unless you have a huge amount to invest. You will never make money on the principal sum you have invested unless inflation stops and interest rates fall. That is so unlikely that it need hardly be considered at all. So you can immediately dismiss municipal bonds, or any bonds at all, as a way to get rich from inflation. They are not at all like real estate or gold or foreign currencies in that regard.

Bear in mind that the tax-free feature of the municipal bond applies only *at the margin,* and this is a crucial fact. If you earn $30,000 a year, you will find that the marginal rate of tax on that sum is perhaps 45 percent. But you will have all kinds of deductions and adjustments to your income so that the amount on which you pay tax is far less than the gross amount. You might pay tax on, say, $18,000. And the marginal rate on that will be far lower, say, 25 percent.

This means that for a person to have a 50 percent tax rate after all his deductions, he would have to have really enormous earnings, far above the middle class. And municipal bond sales are aimed at people whose marginal tax rate is *even higher* than 50 percent.

After all, if the municipal bond pays 6 percent while taxable corporate bonds pay 12 percent, you obviously will only be better off with the municipals if your marginal tax rate is above 50 percent. This magnitude of earnings accrues only to the very rich.

Reason number two why municipal bonds should be avoided is that they have almost monotonically fallen in value for the last ten years. Remember that a bond's price falls as the level of interest rates rise. That means that since interest rates generally move up along with inflation, the prices of bonds generally fall. Municipal bonds are no exception. If inflation continues its merry march, interest rates will continue to rise, and bond prices will continue to fall.

In summary, you will not make much on the interest-free income feature unless you are a Rockefeller, and you will lose money on the principal sum. It is exactly the opposite of what MONEYPOWER is all about.

Stocks and bonds are good for stock and bond brokers. But for the MONEYPOWER investor, there are far greener pastures.

11

New Hedges

MONEYPOWER strategy recognizes that people are different from one another. Some can tolerate far higher levels of anxiety than others. Some have far more time and energy available for the fight against inflation than others. Some have more time and less money and vice versa. Some crave adventure and some crave security.

It is possible that the MONEYPOWER triad of single-family homes, gold futures, and currency trading is unsuitable for many investors. These same investors, nonetheless, may be deeply concerned about inflation.

For them there are a variety of instruments that, while they are not as highly leveraged or as potentially powerful as houses, gold, or currency at beating inflation, nevertheless have major assets for beating inflation. Mostly these instruments are short-term money-market instruments such as Treasury bills and corresponding private-sector units.

The money market is a market very much like the stock market. Borrowers enter the market offering debt instruments and the reaction of the lenders determines what the amount of interest will be on the debt.

In inflationary periods such as the present, money-market rates tend to reflect quite well the rates of inflation plus a small amount. That is, lenders quite naturally refuse to lend their money for less than the going inflation rate over the

short term. If they did otherwise, they would be guaranteed
to lose money.

(Long-term lenders, on the other hand, will sometimes lend
for less than the current inflation rate in the vain hope that
over the period of the loan, the inflation rate will drop below
the coupon rate. This has led, in the current inflationary period,
to a bizarre phenomenon. Usually long-term rates are higher
than short-term rates. The higher rates are intended to induce
lenders to part with their stash for a longer time during which
there is much uncertainty.

(In today's money market though—spring 1979—the long-
term rates are very slightly lower than short-term rates. The
reason is that lenders believe that the inflationary rate is so
high that it will not last. Therefore, they must make more
than the current high inflation rate for the present. Over the
longer haul they have more hope that the coupon rate will
exceed the long-term inflation rate.)

Consequently, short-term money-market instruments yield
good rates of return. The rates will not make the investor
rich, but they will serve him far better than passbook savings.

As of spring 1979, an investor could buy short-term Treasury
notes, redeemable in full in thirteen weeks, paying about 9.5
percent interest. If the notes were for only slightly longer,
namely twenty-six weeks, the yield was about 9.6 percent.

Most established brokerage firms sell the bills with only a
minor commission. The minimum denomination is $10,000.
The bills are not guaranteed by the Federal Deposit Insurance
Corporation or any other such intermediary. They are guaranteed by the federal government itself. There is no better guarantee this side of the pearly gates. If the federal government
becomes unable to honor the obligation, the investor will be
far more worried about radioactive fallout than about inflation.

Recently, under the authority of the federal government,
banks and savings and loans institutions have been authorized

to offer certificates of deposit that are keyed to the current Treasury-bill rate.

Those C.D.'s are usually sold in minimum $10,000 denominations and are guaranteed up to the usual limits by the Federal Deposit Insurance Corporation. Although they do not have the promise of using leverage plus the fundamental forces of inflation to make the investor rich, they keep up rather well with inflation. (That is not the same as outperforming inflation, which they will not do.)

T-bill-geared C.D.'s have the additional advantage of tieing up money for only six months. Even if there are radical changes in the interest rates against you, the price of your C.D. will not change. Moreover, in a short time you can get your money out and reinvest it in a higher-paying instrument.

The new T-bill-pegged C.D.'s show their true worth when compared with previously issued large denomination C.D.'s. Genuinely well-heeled investors can get up to 11 percent on C.D.'s of $100,000 and up for six months to a year. When the investor considers that the return is little better than that for his $10,000 C.D., he might realize that the new T-bill-pegging feature has greatly improved the C.D. interest-rate odds in his favor.

(In addition, many institutions are offering so-called money-market funds. Investors can buy participations for as little as $1,000. The proceeds are invested in government and corporate debt. The yield is something higher than the rate of T-bills. In addition, interest is computed daily. And further, checks can sometimes be written on the balance. But the deposits are not insured. Still, money-market funds bear investigation.)

Treasury bills and bill-pegged C.D.'s will virtually double the passbook return and with no risk. But MONEYPOWER strategy recommends them only for the most cautious and distracted investor. There is simply no way they will make you rich unless you were rich to start with.

MONEYPOWER also notes with caution another form of high-interest investment, which MONEYPOWER does not endorse. Second mortgages are growing in popularity for middle-income investors, with superficially good reason.

A second mortgage on a home or other improvement is a loan secured by the property but with the security interest junior to the security interest of the first mortgage holder. A second mortgage is usually for a small amount of money compared with the first mortgage. Ten thousand dollars is a commonly used amount.

A mortgage broker presumably examines the financial statement and underlying assets of the applicant for the loan. If the loan applicant passes muster, the broker finds a private citizen suitable for lending the money. Suitability means having the money and being willing to part with it for as long as ten years for an interest rate of between 10 and 12 percent in most cases.

The borrower pays not only the 10 percent but also a fee of as much as 15 percent of the principal sum for the broker's services. (Although the alert MONEYPOWER borrower will find, by judicious shopping around, that there are some banks and brokers willing to make the loans with no fee at all.) Then the broker collects the payments and passes them on to the lender.

The lender has, in effect, a ten-year bond with a coupon of 10 to 12 percent. Inasmuch as the security is about as good as the security of a fairly good bond, although certainly not AAA, the similarity is even more marked.

As borrowers have sought to capitalize on the increased equity in their houses—as well they should, for the right investment—brokers have sought to popularize the loans as a form of inflation hedge for the lenders. In fact, they do not fill the bill.

Holding a second mortgage has exactly the same drawback as holding a bond. While the interest rate may seem good today, it is in fact liable to be a few percentage points low by tomorrow's standards. If the coupon rate on your second mortgage is 11 percent, and if the going rate in a few years is 14 percent—as it could well be—your fine investment no longer looks so fine. You will have tied up your money for ten years at a painfully low rate. You will find that if you have to sell your second mortgage to someone else, you will be forced to sell it at a price low enough so that its coupon rate is 14 percent as well. In other words, you will get about 79 cents on the dollar as a penalty for the lower interest rate of your instrument.

Second mortgages are a wonderful invention for borrowers and not for lenders. A borrower can take that money and do something quite exciting with it for a relatively modest rate of interest. The lender is stuck with what may well be a longtime heartbreaker.

As MONEYPOWER has shown, there are several interest-bearing vehicles that have potential as inflation hedges—notably T-bills, and T-bill-pegged C.D.'s. They have the advantage of offering quite high interest rates without tieing up money for long periods.

The latter feature—the short-term nature of the obligation—is crucially important in an era when interest rates are moving so rapidly upward. There is simply no reason to get stuck with high interest rates moving against you because you have a lower-interest-rate, long-term obligation.

MONEYPOWER suggests that if you feel compelled to lend money instead of borrowing it—and MONEYPOWER always prefers borrowing to lending—you should be lending for as brief a time as possible. Do not get caught with your interest rate down while everyone else's is going up. There is nothing in it but frustration.

If you must get into second mortgages, get into them by borrowing with one—not by lending.

And, in general, bear in mind that inflation is a grand opportunity for borrowing. You almost always pay back far less than you borrowed. And it is a time when you can use the borrowed money to make money. The whole meaning of inflation is that prices rise faster than people are prepared for, and therefore you pay back dollars that are worth less than they were when you borrowed them.

The lender subsidizes the borrower in the age of inflation.

Remember that and decide which you want to be: the gift giver or the gift getter.

12

Collectibles: Snare
and Delusion

During times of economic dislocation—such as the present—
when people lose faith in conventional financial instruments,
like money, stocks, and bonds, that faith is often transferred
to unconventional wealth-holding vehicles. A mysterious and
fervent devotion attaches itself to rare collectible items like
rugs, jewels, drapes, pictures, antiques of all descriptions, and
other exotica. Collectively they are called "collectibles" and
today the boom is on in collectibles in a big way.

It is nothing new. Throughout history, people have sought
to hedge themselves against national financial disaster by carrying off and hoarding beautiful relics. Gibbon repeatedly notes
that when pitiful Romans fled city after city in the barbarian
onslaught, they took with them statuary and mosaic works
of art and tapestries in the certainty that they could be exchanged for far more than a comparable weight of the by
then thoroughly debased currency.

During the American Civil War, southern families hid valuable English paintings and French China. Although Confederate
dollars were worthless, sharp hoarders of collectibles exchanged them for vast tracts of land, which are the basis of
major fortunes even today.

After World War II, citizens of the defeated countries found that although their money was close to worthless, they could live well off accumulated art works and historic artifacts.

And today in inflation-riddled America lucky people are finding that collecting rare items, from machine guns to automobiles to paintings to books to coins and everything in between, can yield phenomenal benefits. Every sentient adult has heard wondrous stories about how an item bought at a junk shop has made its owner rich or how a man who collected beer bottles in his basement exchanged them for a steam-driven yacht.

Some of the stories are true. There has been a boom in various kinds of collectibles. Devoted students and collectors in many different fields have found that they can turn their love affairs with various tangible items into mountains of cash. Men and women who have dedicated their lives to learning the most minute details of esoteric fields are occasionally finding that their skill and time has given them valuable assets.

But the true story of collectibles as an inflation hedge is far less cheerful than the occasional fables that come floating into the ears of the gullible innocents of this world. Basically the story on collectibles is this:

Collect for love and make money.

Collect for money and weep.

There are enormous drawbacks in collecting things as a potentially rewarding financial endeavor. For starters, there is a sucker born every minute and two to take him, as P. T. Barnum said. The entire country is crawling with swindlers trying to convince the many suckers of our age that those same suckers, without any expertise, can order all manner of "commemorative" garbage from the pages of magazines and make money on it.

In fact, items that are specifically made to be collectors' items almost never are. The vast array of goodies that certain "mints" and other firms sell through advertisements will never again be worth as much as the eager collector paid for them. They have no intrinsic or social value except to manufacture money for the offering firms. There is no secondary market whatsoever in them as anyone who tries to resell those "valuable collectors' items" has found out.

MONEYPOWER lesson one on collectibles: If it is advertised in a mass-circulation journal as rare and important and potentially valuable, stay away.

Second, collecting tends to go in fads. For instance, around the turn of the century there were crazes for collecting medieval manuscripts. J. P. Morgan and other tycoons collected illuminated manuscripts and other exotic books from all over the world. Staggering prices were paid for them until the early 1920s.

Then the fad abruptly disappeared. Today, those manuscripts will not fetch even a fraction of the prices they received fifty-five years ago. The same has been true of Italian marble statuary. Much beloved in the roaring twenties and even into the 1930s, it has never again brought even what it was selling for during the Depression.

Because collectors' items have little intrinsic value—you cannot eat them or burn them in your car—it is just plain old fad and fancy that makes them valuable. When the fashion passes, the collector is left high and dry.

Collectibles are somewhat like chain letters. As long as the chain keeps going, everyone is fine. But when the chain stops, the last person who paid out the money is in trouble. Connoisseurs of art need only hear the word "geometrics" to know the problem. In the 1960s geometrics—brightly colored cubes and parabolas—were the wave of the future. Astronomical prices were paid for them. Then came the 1970s, and people forgot about geometrics. Now they hang in elegant homes, as dated and worthless (relatively) as Hula Hoops.

Art lovers who appreciate and revere geometrics have no problem at all. They still appreciate them. But men who bought them to make a quick killing got quickly killed.

And this leads to MONEYPOWER's second lesson about collectibles: Beware of fads unless you are deeply in love with
the faddish item and do not care about making money on it.

A third point to remember about collecting is that the market
for collectibles is usually about as liquid as the market for
stolen van Goghs. To find oneself at an auction, whipped into
a frenzy of enthusiasm and confidence that a certain painting
will make one rich and happy is one thing. The auctioneer
will cheerfully accept your money and just as cheerfully turn
over the painting to you.

To try to sell it when you need money is entirely another
thing. There is no organized market for most collectibles such
as the New York Stock Exchange or the Chicago Board Options Exchange. When the time comes to sell, you will have
to try the haphazard methods traditionally associated with
selling a particularly miserable used car.

You can try advertisements in the appropriate journals or
consignment to auctioneers. Or you can sell it directly to a
dealer. But in any case, be prepared for a shock. The auctioneer
will take a fantastic cut of whatever your objet d'art fetches,
sometimes as much as 40 percent. Moreover, even the best,
most prestigious auctioneers will not always be able to sell
your beloved item at once.

If you sell directly to a dealer, do not expect him to offer
you even the wholesale value of your trinket. More likely his
final offer, after the most determined haggling, will be almost—
but not quite—wholesale.

Unless you as a collector are also proprietor of an auction
gallery, you can completely forget about getting the retail price
of your bauble. However much art magazines or kindly friends
tell you your collectors' item has increased in value, do not
expect it to fetch the full amount of retail value.

And that is the catch. You will always pay retail. Even if
you are told that you are not paying retail, you still will be

paying retail, and that is a lot more than wholesale. In other words, you will be buying high and selling low. That leads to MONEYPOWER's third rule of collecting: If you must insist on collecting for money, try to inform yourself about just how you will dispose of your darling toy once the time comes. And never rely on what the salesman tells you about the subject.

The fourth problem with collectibles is that they are subject to wild swings in value even when they are in constant demand. For example, in 1973 gold coins took off on a meteoric rise that hoisted them to almost twice their 1972 levels by the end of 1974. But even while the United States was having 12 percent inflation in 1975, the prices of rare coins took a catastrophic fall. Even excellent specimens lost 60 percent of their value. People who had paid top dollar for glittering prizes could hardly give them away.

For serious numismatists who genuinely loved their coins, the depression in coin prices was only a minor problem. They looked at their coins and lovingly fondled them until the time came, as it surely did in 1977, 1978, and 1979, when the prices came back up again. But for people who hoped to turn the coins into glittering money, there was ashen despair.

The same problems come up even with rare silver pieces and magnificent Aubusson rugs. They will be prized year in and year out, but their prices will fluctuate even if they rise dramatically in the long run.

MONEYPOWER rule number four on collectibles. If you cannot afford to be patient, either financially or temperamentally, stay out of the market altogether.

As the reader can gather, the basic MONEYPOWER guidance on collectibles is to discourage collecting them for purely speculative reasons. Yes, lovers of beauty and lifetime aficionados of even the most esoteric items might well expect to make money on them. In the world of Louis XVI clock collectors there are profits to be made by the Louis XVI clock collector who knows the state of the art better than anyone else or at least as well. And, in addition, the true collector will derive immense psychic pleasure—the most important kind—from his work whether it pays off in cash or not.

But while lovers of collecting will almost always make out, hogs will almost always get slaughtered.

The case of collecting cars for profit is almost a textbook example of just how not to make money and how to be tricked by those who would capitalize on the mania for collecting.

In almost every issue of any automobile magazine there are breathless stories of how such and such a vintage Ferrari is now selling for as much as a city block in lower Manhattan. Pictures of cars march across pages with captions below of prices that might well stagger a Rockefeller. Then stories appear about clunkers from the 1950s that have appeared from a forgetful owner's garage and made the owner as rich as the Sheik of Abu Dhabi.

The MONEYPOWER response to these stories is—hogwash. There are few fields (we will get to one of the others in a moment) in which there is so much trickery and so little substance about prices.

First, the only correct way to assess the prices of cars would be to measure the price set by the forces of supply and demand. In other words, people who sold their cars at auction without reserve as to price would get a true gauge of prices. However, almost no cars are sold at auction without reserve. The most foolish seller is not so foolish as to offer to sell without requiring that a certain reserve price be reached. And only the most poorly sighted person would fail to notice that at many exotic car auctions more than half of the cars do not fetch their reserve price.

Second, a prevalent way of "establishing" the price of a collectors' car is fraught with deceit. Most collectible cars are exchanged through private sales, either between individuals or with a dealer acting on one side as principal or agent. Accurate price information on the cars in these trades is virtually impossible to obtain on any basis. Collectors are usually close-mouthed about the price of a car, wishing to hide either embarrassment or taxable income. Dealers conceal costs and their own profits.

Further, in trades of packages of exotic cars, there is almost no way to figure out the true price. Suppose three fairly exotic cars are exchanged for one very exotic car. Then the parties to the trade, if they are in a publicity-seeking mood, may tell an auto magazine that their cars sold for $100,000 for the most exotic car and an average of $33,000 per for the rather less exotic cars. But who on earth knows if those are the true prices? The parties can assign any price they wish to the package as arbitrarily as they see fit.

In such transactions are $10,000 Volkswagen Baja Buggies made.

A third pitfall for unwary buyers in the collectibles market is the failure to distinguish between real price and nominal price. The real price is the price adjusted for inflation. The nominal price is the price in unadjusted, current dollars.

For example, most Porsches in fairly good condition dating from the 1960s sell for 50 percent more than their original cost—at least. That sounds like just what the alert investor is looking for. But remember that a pound of bread sells for about 100 percent more than it did in the 1960s. So does almost everything else, on average. There lies the rub. Taking the price of an item in dollars unadjusted for inflation is simply meaningless. Although a 1965 Porsche may sell for 50 percent more than its original price, that rise does not even come near to keeping up with inflation.

Of course, most cars do not even sell for as much as they cost originally, so that a car that has risen even in nominal dollars is doing well. But certainly that is no way to keep yourself *ahead* of inflation. Going 50 percent of the distance does not bring you home.

Even the most beautiful and splendid of foreign cars such as Ferraris or Maseratis almost never sell for as much as the initial selling price adjusted for inflation. Yes, there are exceptions, but do not expect to find them unless you have devoted a lifetime to the study and restoration of exotic cars.

Yet another problem with exotic cars is that they are extremely illiquid. It can take a good long while to sell an exotic car. The market for most of them is thin indeed, especially in all but the most heavily populated parts of the country.

If the investor needs to raise money on one in a hurry, he might just as well forget any notions about a good price. A thin market almost always means a weak price and that is true in spades for exotic cars. Occasionally a bank will lend money on an exotic car, but never at the retail price. Be prepared for a shock when you find that the bank's valuation of your dream car is only one-third what yours was.

MONEYPOWER warns the sensible reader that cars are for transportation and for occasional pleasure and somewhat more frequent heartache. No one without a generation's experience in dealing with exotic cars should even expect to escape disaster in dealing with collectible cars for profit. But if the investor loves his car and derives great satisfaction from riding in it and watching the envious stares, if he does not begrudge the eternities that his car will spend in the clutches of rapacious mechanics and body molders, then he will be all right no matter what. If he makes money it is pure gravy. If he does not make money, he had fun anyway.

To recapitulate:

1. It is almost impossible to tell what the real market price of an exotic car is
2. Adjusted for inflation, even high prices for used exotic cars do not seem high except in rare cases
3. There is almost no liquidity in the collectible-cars market
4. The most a sensible person should expect to get out of an exotic, collectible car is pride of ownership

When the MONEYPOWER investor hears a story about a neighbor who put a 1939 Plymouth in his garage forty years

ago and just took it out, then exchanged it for a villa in Cap
d'Antibes, he should smile and pay no mind. The story is
not about cars but about fish.

The problems of inability to tell the real price, liquidity,
and deceit are the common problems of all collectibles. And
while they come out clearly in the case of collectible cars,
they appear even more starkly in the case of a girl's best friend.
Except for having continual demand, diamonds present most
of the problems of collecting with, well, gemlike clarity.

Diamonds are beautiful, rare, and highly prized. Demand
for them will never fall off as it has for geometric paintings
or beaver coats. For as long as they have been around in their
brilliant, polished form, women and some men have loved to
have the cool stones next to their skin.

And, in recent years, the price of diamonds expressed in
dollars has climbed dramatically. Good-quality stones have
doubled from year to year in recent years, at retail, making
some show girls happy. As young couples go into jewelry
stores, they are bowled over by engagement rings that cost
$10,000 a carat. Matrons find that those old stones they had
in jewelry boxes for years are now worth enough to pay off
the estate taxes.

And word gets around that diamonds are the premier inflation hedge. An entire industry has grown up to sell stones
to worried investors as inflation hedges. Glib men in double-
knit suits with their shirts open at the collars and gold chains
around their necks appear at respectable restaurants and tell
their neighbors that they are selling peace of mind in the form
of investment-grade diamonds.

Charts and graphs appear in newspapers and magazines telling people that if they had put $2,000 in diamonds in 1976
they would have $6,000 in 1978. And even the eminent presi-
dents of fine old jewelry establishments take advertisements
to tell readers that diamond prices are unconscionably high.

And, in fact, there is some truth to it all. Diamonds have
been rising in value as inflation rises, only far faster than infla-

tion. But there are red warning signals up all over the field of play about buying diamonds as an inflation hedge.

It is useful at the outset to take some notice of just exactly why diamond prices have gone up so spectacularly. Unfortunately, no one knows the answer exactly, but it apparently has most to do with the diamond-cutting middlemen.

Diamonds come predominantly from mines in South Africa. They are shipped in rough form to diamond cutters who work mostly in Israel, Belgium, and Holland. Those cutters make the diamonds look beautiful. In recent years, they have been concerned about how badly the dollars they take in for their gems have deteriorated in value. As the diamond cutters see it, they pay out X dollars for the diamonds, and then by the time they get paid by the American retailers, even if they get paid 2X, the rapid inflation makes that 2X worth about as much as X a little while before.

So the diamond cutters, as some people say, have withheld diamonds from the market so that the price—following typical principles of supply and demand—will be closer to 4X.

And the diamond cutters' plans have worked perfectly so far. The prices the cutters receive have risen spectacularly as the price in the American market skyrockets.

(There are presumably other reasons for the increase in diamond prices as well. The demand for diamonds in all politically unstable countries is high and there are a lot of politically unstable countries today. Additionally, the huge Japanese market has been opened up to diamond sales. Japanese couples have accepted the innovation of diamond engagement rings in place of the former verbal tokens of love.)

The fact that the price of diamonds has been primarily jacked up by an artificial shortage creates an obvious problem. Someday those diamonds lying around in vaults in Tel Aviv, Brussels, and Amsterdam may come out in a hurry, and diamond prices could go down fast.

Even the cool-headed diamond cutters might someday be

stampeded into unloading the hoard of stones and hammering prices far below current levels.

And this possibility of a sudden increase in demand is enlarged by the reaction of the South Africans to the price rise. Because DeBeers Consolidated Mines, the South African diamond consortium, has been angered by the middlemen's actions, it has recently imposed a surcharge upon its sales to the cutters to encourage them to turn the stones over more quickly. The surcharge does not exhaust South Africa's means of dealing with the diamond cutters. If more pressure is turned on, the diamond cutters may be persuaded to let some of their stones out of the hold.

Those who hawk diamonds as the inflation hedge to end all inflation hedges often claim that diamonds are a better investment than gold because diamonds have no monetary significance. Therefore, the argument runs, no Treasury stands ready to sell diamonds to lower the price of diamonds or raise the price of the dollar. This gives diamonds an upward bias that gold lacks, so the story goes.

But that argument completely disregards the possibility that, for political reasons of its own, South Africa, a volatile commodity in the world of nations, might want to raise a lot of money quickly and might sell diamonds to do it. There is no U.S. Treasury overhang of diamonds, but there is a huge overhang of diamonds in the hands of potentially desperate people.

But that is just the tip of the iceberg of problems with diamond sales that makes diamonds one of MONEYPOWER's least satisfactory inflation hedges.

The diamond market is simply so complex, idiosyncratic, illiquid, and laced with fraud that only the most foolhardy or the most experienced hands should enter it with inflation hedging in mind.

First, as with many collectibles, it is almost impossible to know the correct price. Diamonds are sold on the basis of clarity, brilliance, and other even less tangible factors. Hardly ever will two diamond experts appraise the same stone for the same amount.

Because each stone is unique and each appraisal of it is unique as well, there is an enormous element of uncertainty even under the best circumstances when one tries to price diamonds. If a private citizen without prior expertise in diamonds is offered a quantum of diamonds for a certain price, he simply has no idea at all whether he is paying a good price for them. Even if the buyer is allowed to take the stones to several different jewelers, he will never get exactly the same appraisal on the stones. And in the grim world of investment diamonds, the buyer is rarely allowed to take the diamonds anywhere for appraisal.

(In a recent development that would make Dillinger envious, some "investment counselours" in diamonds have been selling diamonds inside tightly sealed boxes *that the buyer is not allowed to open.* The buyer is promised that there is a ready resale market for the sealed diamonds only if the box is never opened. Fantastic people, those investment counselours.)

Thus the private buyer without investment experience in diamonds is simply buying a pig in a poke. Yes, if the buyer is a longtime friend of a diamond dealer he will likely pay a price that the diamond dealer thinks is fair. But even when a diamond dealer has the best will in the world—which definitely can happen—the price he considers the fair price may differ substantially from what the jeweler next door considers the fair price.

In a word, the unwary investor who seeks to hedge against inflation by buying diamonds has simply no idea at all whether he is buying low or high.

(The very word "hedging" suggests yet another difficulty with diamonds. Because they can rarely if ever be bought with low down payment, long-term credit, they offer the investor no more than their possible, highly speculative appreciation.

There is no leverage to build up the profits to many times what they would be on principal alone. At best, the investor can "hedge"—barely keep up—rather than aggressively grow rich through the forces of borrowing and inflation.)

The inevitable sequel is that the diamond investor must sell low. The problem of illiquidity that applies to almost all collectibles applies in spades to diamonds. Once the diamond investor needs money out of his diamonds, the rest is all too frequently a horror story.

Figure it out: The wholesale price of a diamond is usually 50 percent or less of its retail value. The ordinary investor may be certain that he will pay full retail—at least. But when he goes to a diamond merchant to attempt to sell his stones, he will probably get, as his first offer, a smiling yet grudging offer to pay one-third below wholesale. Only the most rigorous bargaining will get the price up to wholesale. And then you can figure that you have taken a 50 percent loss immediately. It might take a couple of very good years of diamond price rises to bring you out even—let alone ahead—when you buy at retail and sell at wholesale.

Occasionally diamond owners attempt to sell through auctioneers. Some auctioneers are honest and some are not. Even with the very best auctioneer, the diamond owner can expect to pay a good one-third of the price for the auctioneer's services. With a bad auctioneer, the diamond owner is completely at his mercy. The auctioneer can sell the stones at any price, sometimes fraudulently, and the owner is virtually helpless to do anything about it.

Yes, some diamond sellers sell to the gullible with "buy back" guarantees. All too often, though, those guarantees apply only if the customer is going to buy a larger stone. Sometimes they apply only toward paying an alleged "wholesale" price, which turns out to be far less than even real wholesale. (Of course, if the diamond buyer gets such a guarantee from Tiffany, his situation is very comfortable. But the boiler-room operations peddling diamonds at high pressure all around the country are a long way from 57th and Fifth Avenue.)

Moreover, the diamond seller has exactly the same appraisal problem in selling as in buying. If he is offered what sounds like a ridiculously low price for the stone, how is he to know if it is a fair price or not? For all he knows, the price he paid was horribly inflated and the price a buyer offers *him* is perfectly fair. The pricing of diamonds is so subjective that the right price on either end of a transaction is almost impossible to come by.

The amateur investor in diamonds as an inflation hedge is perfectly fair game for the many sharks of the business. They all flock about him in the treacherous waters of illiquidity. And, some might say, he asked for it.

There is yet another problem for the diamond investor. Diamonds are not a perpetual-motion machine. They do not go up forever. In the period from 1959–62, diamonds went into a severe slump. Even top-grade gems fell by more than 25 percent in value. With the present artificial shortage and high prices of diamonds, there is little reassurance that a diamond buyer can have against another drop in diamond prices should that dam in Tel Aviv or Amsterdam ever burst.

The diamond buyer could be hurt badly if diamond prices only fail to rise quite as rapidly. Should the rate of increase slow to even 15 percent a year, a basically healthy amount, the diamond investor will be eaten alive by the difference between the retail buying price and the wholesale selling price. Diamond buyers must have confidence that the present spectacular rise in diamond prices will continue for a few years *just to break even*. Although some may have that confidence, many diamond experts, including DeBeers Consolidated Mines, are working to give them sleepless nights.

If diamonds continue to skyrocket in price, all the problems with appraisal, wholesale selling and retail buying, and illiquidity may come out in the wash. If there is even a slight slow-down, there will be major trouble.

(To be fair, there are two circumstances in which buying diamonds is sensible. First, if you have a genuinely close connection in the diamond business, diamonds might make sense. If you have a person whom you can trust to buy and sell at fair prices, who can give completely objective appraisals, and can advise you without partiality on the ins and outs of the diamond business, then the price rise in diamonds can be converted into money in your pocket.

(Second, completely and totally separate from their value as an inflation hedge, diamonds have some value as a disaster survival tool. If you believe that the days of western civilization are numbered, diamonds may be a good friend. If the day comes when paper money is worthless, mobs may well be roaming the streets. Gold and diamonds may be the only passports to security and even to the necessities of life. But again, remember that this is not a MONEYPOWER inflation-beating use.)

The same problems that apply to collectibles in general apply to cars and diamonds:

- No clear market value in either selling or buying
- A highly idiosyncratic and unpredictable behavior of demand
- Extreme illiquidity in both buying and selling, raising the buying price and lowering the selling price
- The unfortunate presence of unscrupulous operators

Yes, if you see the Aubusson carpet that you must have, buy it. If you have always wanted a 1962 Corvette and now is your chance to drive one, drive one. If your bride deserves the biggest little diamond you can find, get it. But buy for love. Then if you make money, it is all gravy. When you try to buy beauty for money, you are likely to find sorrow at the end of the rainbow.

13

College Costs: Make
Inflation Pay

One of the most controversial investments of recent years has been a college education. In nominal dollars, a college education has gotten to be extremely expensive, with a year at an eastern college sometimes costing over $8,000 a year as this is written. Even at state universities, the cost, including plenty of allowance so that junior will not be embarrassed in front of his friends, can run to $5,000 a year.

And as the cost of going to college rises, more and more people question the utility of going to college. Perfectly intelligent people question whether colleges teach the kinds of disciplines that once made college so useful. Perhaps, some say, colleges have become so enmeshed in the effort to become relevant that there is no particular value in giving junior a four-year vacation, which will end with him knowing how to disco dance and criticize movies.

And in strictly economic terms there is growing question about the value of a college degree. There is no doubt at all that the college graduate tends to earn more than the high-school graduate in the American economy. Government statistics show that about 18 percent of American families are headed by college graduates, but those 18 percent account for close to 45 percent of all the families with gross incomes above $30,000.

Even more seemingly relevant, the average college graduate earns about $250,000 more in current dollars than the average non-college graduate over the course of his working life.

In reply, some say that the people who could go to college and graduate successfully can make even more money than college graduates by simply putting their good sense, which would have been twisted in college, to work before it gets a chance to become confused. And there are those with a strictly statistical bent who point out that if you gave a student the cost of his college education and put it in trust for him at interest, he would come out far better than if the money was thrown down the maw of an academic bureaucracy. Say, $25,000, at only 7 percent interest, would yield $250,000 within thirty-four years. Thus, when junior was, say, fifty-six years old, he could have $250,000 all in one lump even with inflation, which he might be able to use far better than a few more dollars in his paycheck every week.

Still, despite all the questions, there is no doubt that a college education is still a good investment. And certainly at this stage of investigation of the relative merits of a college education, MONEYPOWER wholeheartedly recommends a college education as an intelligent inflation-beating investment.

And a college education fits the clearest MONEYPOWER requirements for an inflation-defeating vehicle:

- It can be highly leveraged
- Its return outperforms the rate of inflation
- It comes with many government subsidies
- The market for it is extremely liquid

Before one can understand just how perfectly a college education fits into the MONEYPOWER scheme of things, a college education must be looked at in the proper perspective. A college education is not a device for enhancing the social status of parents. Nor is it a medium for giving a child access to revealed wisdom and serenity. A college education is an investment in improving the efficiency of a productive resource—namely a human being. That is a cool way of describing it, but it is the only sensible way. (If you look at it as anything more elevated, you are looking for heartbreak.)

If a college education is correctly understood as very much akin to a new factory or a drill press, the next question is, who owns the productive factor? Certainly not the parents, who will be lucky to see a penny of the increased production of their child. The obvious answer is that the child is the owner of his own increased productivity. As such, a simple conclusion can be drawn: The student should pay for his own college education.

And indeed, MONEYPOWER postulates that if the student pays for his own education, and does it with borrowed money, then and only then is real MONEYPOWER progress being made.

It is just as logical for a student to pay for his own education as for General Motors to pay for its own new stamping plant. However, unlike General motors, the student can pay for his own education with long-term, no-down-payment, low-interest, government-subsidized loans. There is a plethora of programs underwritten by Uncle Sam that allow the student to pay for a huge portion of his college education with loans at interest rates that no one else in the country could even dream of.

And best of all, the student can pay off his loans when the dollars to pay them off are plentiful. He borrows valuable dollars and pays back cheap dollars. Here is how it works.

Suppose Joe Doaks wants to send his daughter Sandy off to Oklahoma University. He has quite rightly decided that she should pay for part of the cost through summer jobs, part through part-time work at school, and most through loans. The Doakses are a middle-income family bringing home about $24,000 a year. They are therefore eligible for the Guaranteed Student Loan program. Many banks and credit unions offer them (although many banks have become fed up with the paper work and do not offer them). The federal government underwrites the loans. At this writing a Guaranteed Student Loan can offer up to $2,500 a year, at 7 percent interest (!), payable over the course of a maximum of ten years. The bank's excess costs over the 7 percent interest rate are borne by the federal government.

The simple fact is that with such low interest and such a long time to repay the loan, a college education has become a prime bargain in the age of inflation. Even though inflation has raised the cost of a college education sky-high, the inflation of the future will raise paychecks by so much that repayment will require a trifling fraction of the college grad's wages.

Facts and figures: Suppose that little Sandy Doaks borrows a total of $8,000 for all four years of college under the Guaranteed Student Loan program. Her monthly payment to pay off interest and principal will be about $93. Suppose that she does not get any degrees beyond her B.A. and receives a starting salary of $1,400 a month when she graduates in 1982. (In fact, starting salaries for college graduates are about $1,000 a month in 1978, and a $1,400 starting salary four years hence assumes modest, but not horrendous, inflation.) Assuming that she has deductions of about 30 percent of her salary, she will take home about $980 a month. That means that in the first year, she will pay about 9.5 percent of her take-home pay for repayment of the loan.

But, in the recent past real wages of workers between the ages of twenty-one and forty-five have risen by about 7 percent per year. That means the nominal wages have risen by about 7 percent *plus* the current rate of inflation. If we imagine that Sandy is a typical wage earner and that inflation runs about 9 percent per year, a modest expectation, then Sandy's wages will rise by about 16 percent per year. After two years as a wage earner, Sandy's pretax earnings will be about $1,880 dollars. Her after-tax slice will be about $1,316, assuming that her total deductions rise by only a trifling amount. That means that her $93 college loan repayment will be only about 7 percent of her take-home pay.

In five years after graduation, Sandy's monthly wage will be almost $2,900, assuming 10 percent inflation, and assuming that her deductions are now 35 percent of her salary, her net monthly pay will be $1,900. Her repayment will take only about 4.8 percent of her take-home pay.

And so it goes. By the last year of her repayment term, Sandy's take-home pay will be over $3,500 a month. Her paltry $93-a-month repayment amount will be only about 2.6 percent of her net pay.

A few facts are worth noting. First, the reason Sandy's pay seems so phenomenally high is that we are denominating it in current dollars, unadjusted for inflation. And if that seems still too high, bear in mind that the average family in America grosses close to $20,000 a year in 1979. Remember when that seemed like a rich man's salary?

Second, Sandy will not be rich with the salaries stated above. Everything will cost a lot more than it does now. The loan repayment amounts, however, will not change. They are fixed by contract.

Everyone in the world knows that those dollars are not at all the same dollars that they were back when Sandy Denman took out her loan. They are more like quarters were then. But the bank will continue to accept them as if they were just as good as ever.

Result: Sandy Doaks has borrowed expensive dollars, bought a valuable productive asset—her college education—and repaid cheap dollars. And this is exactly why a college education is custom made for long-term financing in the age of inflation.

Not everyone can get loans under the Guaranteed Student Loan program. Before MONEYPOWER gets to those people, let's consider low-income people. Many of them are eligible for an even better subsidized loan program called the National

Direct Student Loan program. Under that scheme, students and their families must show financial need. Sometimes that is hard to do and sometimes not. It largely depends upon the standards of vigilance of your college loan officer.

But if you can qualify for this program, you can get government-subsidized loans made directly through the Department of Health, Education, and Welfare at 3 percent. That kind of interest rate cannot be beat anywhere in the world today. It is as close as you can get to an interest-free loan. And in the era of continuous high inflation, an interest-free loan— or a 3 percent loan—is an outright gift. The monthly payments are so small, and get to be even smaller so fast, that they become negligible within a couple of years after graduation.

However, some families do not qualify for government-subsidized loans because of their incomes—too high—or because of their assets—too much. Sometimes these families can get loans subsidized by their state governments. The regulations and the interest rates vary dramatically over both time and space. But your bank will have an idea of just what the situation is with regard to state-subsidized loans. Even if the subsidy does not reduce the interest rate to 7 percent, snap up that loan. It will definitely be worth your while. Any subsidy that lowers an interest rate at a time when interest rates are already lower than they should be is well worth taking on.

Some families will not qualify for any kind of subsidized loan, however. Their question is whether they should borrow to pay for a college education without the loan being subsidized. The answer is—almost always—yes.

Many banks offer students "lines of credit" for college costs. These loans are usually the legal responsibility of the parents. It is then the responsibility of the parents to get the kids to pay for the loans in point of fact. In the fall of 1978, bank lines of credit for students in New York and California were costing from 13 to 15 percent.

Here is where second-order analysis is crucial. To the uninformed, and interest rate of 13 to 15 percent appears to be painfully high. But, in fact, each 1 percent difference in the interest rate means only a small amount on a loan of the size MONEYPOWER refers to. For example, on a loan of $8,000 amortized in equal monthly installments over ten years, each 1 percent increase in the interest rate means an additional payment per month of between $4 and $5. In the scheme of things, with inflation raising a typical college graduate's monthly pay by more than $160 in the first year alone, a few dollars more per month for that college education is nothing.

Until interest costs for a college loan reach the point where they exceed the added value of the college education compounded by inflation, any long-term loan is worthwhile to pay for college. (For all practical purposes, no one need expect such a high interest rate—above 20 percent—in the immediate future.)

The exact opposite of what MONEYPOWER prescribes is to be afraid that a student will be weighed down by having an immense lump of indebtedness to work off as soon as he or she graduates from college. Nothing could be further from the truth.

The graduating student whose family has followed the MONEYPOWER strategy has no such problem. He has

- a small monthly payment,
- which rapidly gets smaller
- as inflation generates more nominal dollars in his pocket, and
- the college education the loan paid for raises his real income.

There are three good pieces of advice about college in the age of inflation:

- The student should pay for his own education
- He should do it with loans as much as possible
- Borrowing for college is not a burden, but a privilege

The same rules of borrowing for education apply to higher degrees, which will clearly yield more income, such as law school, medical school, business school, and so forth. For graduate schools that yield benefits in a knowledge of esoteric but poorly paid fields, the MONEYPOWER calculus does not apply. Graduate schools in Sanskrit or German poetry come under the general rubric of collectibles. Do it for love, but do not expect money.

And if all of the foregoing seems complicated, simply remember this: If your kids must go to college, do your utmost to get a subsidized loan or any reasonable loan at all, and make sure the graduate pays for it.

14

A Summary on Investment

And now, with the final words on college as an investment, MONEYPOWER comes to the end of the line on the investing portion of the MONEYPOWER strategy. Before MONEYPOWER goes forward into the correct approach to earning and spending to beat inflation, a few summary words on investments are necessary.

The three prime inflation-beating vehicles listed earlier—houses, gold, and foreign currencies—are MONEYPOWER's top-of-the-line models for the age of inflation. MONEYPOWER does not claim that they are the best vehicles for profits in all situations and for all people. There are many fine investments that lack nothing in appeal but are simply not ideal for capitalizing on *inflation.*

In some parts of the country, stores selling ski equipment must be a fantastic investment. In other parts of the country, stores selling nursing equipment must be even better. An infinity of special situations for making profits exists in this great country, and MONEYPOWER does not for a moment claim to have cornered the market on them. MONEYPOWER's investments are aimed at a specific theme of American life that affects everyone—inflation. MONEYPOWER does not presume to tell the reader that its investments are better than a wonderful situation he has happened into or developed.

Yes, stocks are a bad investment in general as an inflation

beater. But also yes if someone offers you a great deal of a very hot stock at the offering price—go get it. Yes, multi-unit dwellings can be millstones if rent controls are slapped on. But also yes if you have a chance to build one in Fort Lauderdale and cash out with 100 percent profit, using all bank money—do it.

MONEYPOWER recommendations are for the man who does not have those lucky breaks falling into his lap. MONEYPOWER is for everyone who sees inflation and wants to capitalize on it and has no "insider" situations that might be preferable. The rules of MONEYPOWER are about inflation. They are not meant to exclude all other situations from your purview.

There are many forces at work in the American economy to develop profits. Inflation is the most prevalent and most powerful. But there are others.

Even as inflation-beating vehicles, the three main MONEY-POWER recommendations should not be considered as the complete encyclopedia. There are many other opportunities around to turn a national disaster into a personal fortune.

Some people have gotten rich quick by playing with interest-rate futures. These are contracts to buy and sell large quantities of government bonds. As interest rates fluctuate, the price of the contracts can change dramatically overnight. In general, the prices of the contracts go down as interest rates rise. And, in theory, interest rates will rise as inflation rises. Therefore, also in theory, the man who sells interest-rate futures short will tend to make money. But MONEYPOWER does not go into interest-rate futures because they are simply too esoteric. The entire subject of just how long-term interest rates will behave given varying short-term rates of inflation or varying weekly growths of the money supply is richly complex. We know that in the long run inflation makes interest rates rise, but the short-term behavior of interest rates is even more tricky than the behavior of foreign-currency options. And that is *too* tricky. Even brilliant academics debate the question. If it is that exotic, it is too risky for the average, even the brave average, investor. Hence, it bears no MONEYPOWER endorsement.

There are many other speculative vehicles that have made money for investors. Deep discount convertible bonds, bonds without good Standard & Poor's ratings, and bonds of cities with credit problems—such as New York City—can offer extremely good yields. The problems with these instruments, though, are many. If Standard & Poor's has given a bond a low credit rating, that may be a warning to the wise about just how likely the investor is to receive the promised high rate of interest. Questions about whether the bond will ever pay off at par may also be implied.

Similarly, if convertible debentures are selling at a deep discount, there may be questions about just how reliable the payoff performance of the issuing company is. Although these investments could quite possibly pay off handsomely if the issuer's prospects improve, the whole escapade is a risk-taking venture having little to do with the underlying forces of inflation, which is what MONEYPOWER is all about.

Some federally sponsored bond-issuing agencies offer indebtedness that pays off even better than Treasury bills. Export-Import Bank notes, obligations of the District of Columbia Armory Board, and other little-known instruments can offer yields half a point or more above the prevailing rate for Treasury bills. Some of these obligations are backed by the full faith and credit of the United States government (the best guarantee there is) and some are not. There are simply too many of them and the yields fluctuate too quickly for MONEY-POWER to give a comprehensive brief on them. They are quicksilver instruments, and if the investor catches them at the right moment they can yield good rewards as hedges. (Note: They will not offer the phenomenal prospects for making real money that more highly leveraged investments offer. They will help you keep up with inflation but will hardly put you ahead.)

As with all fixed-interest instruments though, there is the ever-present danger of what once seemed like a good yield turning into a poor yield if the interest rate rises dramatically.

Remember that a rising interest rate will force down your debt-instrument price and leave you sorry.

Also remember that in time of inflation it is far better to be a borrower than a lender.

Also remember that even the three most highly recommended MONEYPOWER investments—houses, gold, and foreign currencies—involve some risk. The man who has only a limited amount of capital and a fixed income should be extremely wary of getting himself into a situation in which he must lie awake worrying each night about where his next mortgage payment will come from. There is no profit in putting yourself through psychic torments to make money.

Gold and foreign currencies can fluctuate dramatically even from day to day. There is no sense in getting involved in them if you will become a nervous wreck watching the quotations hour by hour. Yes, the long-term trends of inflation will make a lot of money for the man with staying power and a cool head. But there can be protracted short-term periods when the dollar rallies against both gold and Swiss francs. Read the chapters on these subjects carefully. Never buy gold or foreign currencies as the United States heads into a recession or Switzerland, Germany, or Japan heads into a major inflation. Be informed about what you put your money into, or you will come out well educated but sorry.

Houses are illiquid. Make certain that you have a reserve of money in a highly liquid form for emergencies. Even the most cautious, studious investor will have a hard time finding a bank account that pays enough to keep up with inflation, but it is essential to have cash on hand. (There are plans, however, that pay high interest and give free checking and other services. These free extras may add up to a considerable bonus, which may go a long way to getting a truly meaningful yield from your bank deposit. It is not true that all banks offer the same interest rates and services. Look into it.)

Several brokerage firms now offer money-market funds that pay high rates of interest—equal usually to T-bill rates—and allow the writing of checks on them. They fear investigation, as mentioned above.

Even if your house reaches a market value of twice what you paid for it in short order, should you become ill and need surgery, you will have to pay for it with money. It is always wise to stretch both resources and imagination to make money. It is always foolish to put yourself on the rack of lean times while your houses grow rich. Land-poor is almost as bad as poor if you need the money immediately. Yes, given a little time you can borrow on your house. But for immediate emergencies, nothing takes the place of money in the bank.

Above everything else, remember that MONEYPOWER advice is general and personal lives are specific. If you live in a rooming house on social security and have $10,000 in the bank, forget about speculations in houses or gold or currencies. If you are a young man making a good wage and are socking money away, you are a fool not to put it to good MONEYPOWER advantage. And there are many situations in between in which the MONEYPOWER advice on making inflation work for you *plus* good common sense will create a worry-free future.

You, the ordinary citizen, can definitely beat inflation. The people who are doing it are only different from you in that they do it and you do not. But you must visualize yourself doing it and then you must do it before it will get done. And it must be done with good common sense about who you are, what you have to lose and to gain, and what you cannot afford to lose.

PART THREE

Behavior Modification: The Inflation School and Its Lessons

15

Work for Yourself, Young Man

For most of us, work is a necessity of life. We simply have to do it to earn enough money to put Branola on the table. Even if we have enough capital and borrowing power to get started on the MONEYPOWER program of acquiring property or gold futures or currency options, we rarely have enough money so that we can simply live off the income from the money.

And so, we have to work. But the grim facts are that in the age of inflation all too many of us get no richer from working. Many of us hardly even keep up with the game. The game is inflation and the rising cost of living. Certainly that does not mean we should stop working. We must work to live—at least most of us—and not working puts us farther behind than working.

But the MONEYPOWER reader should be under no illusions that working automatically keeps him even with inflation, or that he is still getting in on the legend of the ever-increasing American standard of living. The sad but true fact is that, since hyperinflation began in 1968, the real spendable earnings of almost half of the American workers in almost every sector have declined.

After allowance for inflation and taxes, the standard of living of about 45 percent of American workers has failed to rise and has even dipped slightly in the last decade. The 1968–78 decade of hyperinflation has marked the most severe loss of growth and the longest stagnation of living standards since the Great Depression.

So much for the idea that while prices are going up, wages are going up even faster. The wage earner who wants to keep his head above water cannot count on his wages to do it. They will go up, but not automatically as fast as inflation.

At this point some readers will stop and say to themselves, "Well, I have nothing to worry about because my union has graciously provided me with a cost-of-living escalator in my contract."

Alas, there may be a COL clause in your contract, but if you are looking for it to keep you up with inflation or ahead or it, you are likely to be disappointed.

Here's how that works—or does not work. About 25 million Americans are covered by cost-of-living clauses in their contracts for employment. Most of these contracts run along the lines of giving a 1-cent-per-hour wage increase for every .3 percent rise in the Consumer Price Index. If a worker's base hourly wage is $8, which is a modest figure for the manufacturing unions, then each 1-cent-per-hour increase is one-eighth of 1 percent of the worker's hourly wage.

Obviously, if the cost of living rises by three-tenths of a percent, and the worker's wage rises by one-eighth of a percent, there is something not keeping up with something else. The worker's cost of living is rising .3 percent and the worker's compensation is rising .12 percent. The cost of living is getting way ahead.

If the worker's basic wage is $10 per hour, he will fall still farther behind under a typical cost-of-living clause in a contract. Then, if a .3 percent rise in the CPI generates a 1-cent rise in pay per hour, the worker is getting exactly .1 percent boost in pay for every .3 percent boost in the cost of living. There is no way the worker can keep up.

But most union pay settlements also call for one- or two-shot pay increases of substantially more per hour to keep the worker's wages up with inflation. The problem is that the wages generally simply cannot rise enough to keep up with inflation even with those lump-sum jumps in pay. Although the union will do its best to get a pay increase that will protect the worker against inflation, the union will rarely succeed.

In the era of rapidly rising prices and stagnant productivity, there simply is not enough money to go around to pay for all those wage increases that everyone wants and deserves. The employers are not being cruel to the workers and good to the stockholders. Most of them simply are not making enough money to shield everyone from the whirlwind of inflation. And the economy in general is not operating at a high enough level of efficiency to provide enough wages to keep a workingman ahead of inflation.

If that sounds hard to believe, imagine the United States as a Latin American banana republic. The banana republic has to import everything it needs from countries that are efficient, and whose money is worth something. So everything the banana republic imports is extremely expensive. The workers in the banana republic work hard, but young rich kids in the banana republic keep the banana-republic workers from using new machinery for fear that it will harm the tropical jungle. So the workers do not get paid much and everything the workers have to buy is expensive.

On top of that, the generalissimo who runs the banana republic is not popular. To make people like him, he prints money at a frantic pace. That puts a lot of money in circulation, but no one is producing anything more, so all of that money goes into higher prices.

If you keep that image of the Unites States in your mind, you will get a clearer idea of just why the American economy cannot pay all its workers enough to keep them ahead of inflation.

In that case, what can a worker do to keep his family afloat on the seas of inflation? To be fair, some unions have wage agreements that give them wage increases greater than the cost of living. Those unions are mainly in the government area.

While other workers have been looking for the Hamburger Helper, the civil servants of America have been eating filet mignon. The wages of these workers are adjusted for inflation, *and* for supposed productivity increases—a bad joke—*and* for increases in wisdom and skill based upon outstanding merit and seniority, which is even more of a bad joke.

And, in fact, MONEYPOWER advises that if a worker must work for someone else, he should do his utmost to find a slot in the federal bureaucracy. The pay is excellent and the security is perfect. And most important of all, the government cannot quantify how much productivity it gains or loses. Governmental units do not have to show a profit, after all. They operate not on the basis of the quality of their product or the efficiency of their service, but on the basis of how much money they can wring out of the American people by compulsion of law.

Because the law operates to dragoon the American people into paying progressively higher amounts of their progressively more worthless incomes in tax because of the progressive tax structure, the government is the only enterprise in America that operates more and more richly as there is more inflation.

(Figure it out. If a worker makes $10,000 and is in the 17 percent tax bracket as an average, he pays $1,700 in tax. If that worker's wage goes up to $20,000, he will find himself perhaps in the 22 percent average tax-bite level. He will pay $4,400 in tax.

(Because of inflation, that $20,000 wage is equal to slightly less than the $10,000 wage was ten years before. But the progressive tax system treats it as if it were an increase in the worker's real wealth, and taxes him on it at a far higher rate. This is bad for the taxpayer but good for the tax collector. The government's real take has increased rapidly, while the real living standard of the worker has declined. Of such machinations are enormous government salaries made.)

If a person has to work for someone else, he might just as well work for someone who will not feel the constraints of inflation but will instead feel the benefits of inflation. That is Uncle Sam.

Unfortunately, or perhaps fortunately, not everyone is suited to work for the government. More important, being a civil servant will keep you barely ahead of inflation, but it will not yield the enormous compounded increments in wealth that the MONEYPOWER investor craves.

MONEYPOWER suggests that on the earnings side every inflation-sensitive person must make a substantial effort to put himself into a position in which he can control his own wage. In simple terms, you must make every effort to work for yourself. Only those who set their own prices and wages can capitalize on inflation not only in investments, but also in earnings.

For those who have the courage to strike out on their own, the era of continuous inflation can be heaven on earth. The entire meaning of continuous inflation is that consumers expect prices to be higher whenever they go to a mechanic or a painter or a watch repairman or a dress shop. If there is one fact of life that has benefited the independent operators of America, it is the almost complete removal of psychic barriers to higher prices.

On the other hand, the costs of the solo operator will be higher as well. The costs of rent, materials, taxes, labor, and everything else will rise rapidly. Where, then, is the opportunity for profit?

The opportunity arises because, while the economy as a whole cannot raise its productivity because of a straitjacket of legalistic controls, individual operators can raise their productivity. They can work harder and more efficiently. They can become more skilled at their work. They can produce more faster. They can make each unit of their time bring in more money even faster than wages and other costs are hitting them. They can invest in themselves, become insiders investing in a productive factor of which they have unique and special knowledge—themselves.

While a Consolidated Edison may be prevented by a variety of legalisms from building a new generator that would make better use of coal or oil, a car mechanic will not be forced to work less hard when he is working for himself. Of course, the government will impose other constraints and barriers to his ingenuity, but the mechanic can still manage to fix a few more carburetors when he is working for himself than when he was working for the Ford dealership.

Although you as an individual workman at a large enterprise cannot raise your pay above the average of the shiftless lot who work with you, you as an individual working for yourself can raise your pay to the exact level of your productivity. Similarly, if your work thrives and you hire help to work with you, you can by threats and promises raise the productivity of those who work with you. You personally can explain to your helpers that they are not allowed to simply serve time. Once they understand that their work and continued employment are intimately connected with their productivity, they will either quit or will generate still more income for you.

Bear it in mind: Just because the United States as a whole is sinking to the level of a banana-republic economy, there is nothing stopping you personally from seizing the day and making money by working for yourself. There are plenty of wealthy men and women in Guatemala.

Once again, the inflationary era provides the golden moment for individual entrepreneurs on a small level. By definition, the economy is suffering from a shortage of people who can and will do anything right. If you come along in any area, however esoteric and rarefied, and show you can do the job at a price short of angina pectoris, you have a lock on fortune. And the constant consumer expectation of higher prices helps smooth out the bumps in the road. Customers will look for someone who will do the job. Price considerations are so fluid and mushy that a beginner does not have to meet the prices of the established, poorly functioning enterprises. The beginner—you—just has to do it right.

Also, MONEYPOWER prescribes owning and operating your own business as a principal way of acquiring financial independence. One of the absolutely most vital elements of modern American life is that an entrepreneur can still create a profitable venture and sell it out for a multiple of profits. He can then take the money and live off it for the rest of his life.

You cannot sell your labor as a wage slave *except on a periodic basis while you are actually working.* That precludes ever achieving financial independence.

Watch how it works to understand just how important owning a business can be in the capitalist society.

Suppose you are a painter. You start a business painting houses and other buildings. Gradually it starts to make money. It makes, after a decent interval of mortification, $50,000-a-year profit. You have long since stopped working with a brush yourself. Instead, you have a little office where you assign jobs and persuade people to pay their bills. The business brings in $50,000 profit whether you are there or not.

Along comes someone with money to invest, looking for a return of $50,000 a year. He sees your business. The two of you dicker and then decide that it would be perfectly fair for you to get a price of ten times earnings for your business.

That means that your little painting business will land $500,000 in your bank account. You can take that, put it into 9.5 percent Certificates of Deposit, and have about $47,500 a year to live on for a while. Or you can put it into property and take capital-gains income that keeps up with inflation. In any event, you have the money. You do not have to be at the painting office any longer. You have only to take the money and do with it what you will.

Let us imagine on the other hand that you are a wage slave, even a highly paid wage slave. You take your high wage and spend it on season tickets to the Rams. Suppose that you have put in the years, and your yearly wage is an excellent $50,000. You are paid the wage in return for your labor.

You can never, not ever, capitalize your wages and sell them. You can never sell the labor of yourself and go to live on an island in the sun. If you are not working, there are no wages to sell. The situation of the wage slave is completely different from the situation of the independent businessman. The former has no capital to sell except his own labor. He will have to work until he acquires capital through the MONEYPOWER process or until he retires.

The businessman can capitalize the earnings of the business and sell it whether he is there or not. That is a major difference. MONEYPOWER tells us that in a capitalist society a man must have capital. Unless he has something that yields earnings aside from his own labor:

- he is condemned to a lifetime of unremitting toil
- at wages that will not keep up with inflation, and
- he has nothing to leave to his posterity to ease their journey through a difficult life.

Note well that the entrepreneurial spirit of American society is rapidly fading. Large enterprises and large government steadily suck the blood of individual initiative. Powerful segments of society are hostile to the free-enterprise spirit. Government regulations make the creation of new businesses steadily more difficult and painful.

MONEYPOWER notes the trend and warns that the day may not be far off when the American climate is terminally unhealthy for the growth of new small businesses. In some nearby future era we may all be wage slaves, dependent upon our earnings and our savings—utterly amazed that a time ever existed when a man could start a business, capitalize its earnings, and make his children and his children's children financially secure for life.

The lesson is short and sweet: Get it while you can.

Working for yourself is the only sensible way to beat inflation in your work. A golden moment exists when the ordinary citizen can take advantage of the capitalist system to capitalize on his labor and his ingenuity. It may not last long.

The golden moment is made more brilliant because in the age of continuous inflation, working for yourself is the best way to invest in something that may become a fabulously productive factor known only to you—you. Yes, you can stay about even by the narrow expedient of working for the government. But if your goal is not just to keep barely above water, but to wring every morsel of advantage out of inflation and yourself—work for yourself.

16

Credit Cards: An
Underrated Friend

"Getting and spending we lay waste our powers." So said the poet Wordsworth. And he wrote in a period of price stability. In the era of continuous inflation, rising prices, ever increasing above any sensible level based on expectation and experience, lay waste our energies and our hopes.

The major part of the MONEYPOWER strategy says that the ordinary citizen can use inflation to his advantage, can use it, in fact, to make himself rich—even by inflationary standards. He can do that by borrowing to buy assets that rise in value far faster then the rate of inflation plus the cost of the borrowing.

There is a corollary to that strategy on the spending side. When the needs of human life dictate that something must be bought as a physical or psychic necessity, there is a more sensible way to go about it—a MONEYPOWER way.

Buying in the age of hyperinflation can and must be done with the aid of borrowing. That is the only surefire way to make it work for you instead of against you. And the most sensible, most legitimate way of borrowing to shop is called a credit card.

There has been more nonsense written about credit cards

than about almost any other modern subject. In one woman's magazine after another, supposed experts tell women that they should hide their credit cards and not use them. Articles in otherwise sensible financial journals tell readers that the use of credit cards is simply wrong, as a matter of both national economic policy and as a matter of good sense.

In fact, used properly, credit cards are the godsend that consumers need in periods of continuing inflation. A credit card is a means of getting immediate credit for any kind of purchase covered by the store that honors your credit card. In general the interest on the debt you have thus incurred is payable as follows. If you pay your credit-card bill within a brief time after its receipt, you need pay no interest at all. If you take a longer time to pay, interest charges are generally imposed against the unpaid balance of your bill at the rate of 1½ percent per month. Each month you are given the option of cutting off any further interest payments by simply paying the remaining balance.

The confusion over the proper function of credit cards generally arises from the simpleminded assumption that since the interest charge is 1½ percent per month, and since there are twelve months in a year, you are paying 18 percent interest. In some fallacious explanations of how the process works, innocent people are told that if they buy an item that costs $100 and pay for it with a credit card, they will wind up paying $118 for it because of the alleged 18 percent interest rate.

In fact, that is not the way it works at all. If the MONEY-POWER shopper looks at credit-card shopping as an opportunity to save money—which it is—the facts turn out entirely differently and far more appealing.

A credit card is first and foremost a way of bridging difficult periods with small loans at low interest rates. If a housewife sees that for one brief moment there is a sale at her local furniture store, and that the inflationary march of prices on the sofa she needs has temporarily stopped and even retreated, she can buy even if she does not have the money in her hand. She can get instant, unquestioned credit to buy that sofa at the sale price. If she pays her bill within the specified period, that extension of credit costs her nothing.

Look at it with numbers.

Mrs. Smart sees the sofa of her dreams on sale for $500. It usually costs $600. Next month, after the sale, the same sofa will cost $700. Mrs. Smart has used most of her money to buy houses and so she needs to use her credit card to buy the sofa. Out comes her Master Charge or Visa. She buys the sofa and it is hers.

She has now saved at least $100, and perhaps as much as $200, which is either 17 percent or 29 percent depending on how you compute it.

If Mrs. Smart pays her bill right away, she has her savings net of any interest costs. She has defeated the high cost of inflation in furniture (furniture is one of the fastest-rising items in the Consumer Price Index of the last few years) even though she had no ready cash.

Thus her credit card has been just what it is supposed to be—a bridge to tide the temporarily cashless over ebbs in the inflationary current.

Suppose Mrs. Smart cannot pay her bill right away. In fact, suppose that she can pay only $50 of it in the first month of the bill. Thus her unpaid balance is $450. The first month's interest charge on it will be only $6.75. If Mrs. Smart pays off the rest of her indebtedness after the first month, she will have incurred only $6.75 in interest for the use of that money *at exactly the moment when she needed it.*

But even if we suppose that Mrs. Smart pays off her sofa debt slowly at the rate of $50 of principal each month, her average indebtedness over the course of ten months will have been $250. Her total interest will have been only $37.50. That means that her total interest as a fraction of the amount she originally borrowed will have been only 7.5 percent. (Since there is compounding involved, the actual calculations are slightly different.)

And this is crucial. The alert MONEYPOWER consumer must ignore the fact that credit cards carry an annual percentage interest charge of 18 percent. That is simply an irrelevant number for almost any purpose. The relevant number is how much money you actually pay in interest for the use of that card and for buying the things you want and need.

In general, the actual interest cost is far smaller than 18 percent of the total you have paid simply because the interest is assessed against a constantly declining balance.

More to the point, examine Mrs. Smart's situation. She got her sofa at an enormous savings during a lull in the inflationary tide, and she paid an interest cost that was trivial compared to her savings.

Even if Mrs. Smart had taken the absolutely longest time she could have taken to pay off her sofa, which would have exceeded two years, her interest costs would still have been less than her savings—less than 50 percent of her savings as a matter of fact.

And the stretching-out feature of credit-card payments is another plus for them as an inflation-beating weapon. As the time for repayment is extended and as inflation mounts in the period of repayment, the true interest costs diminish even further. For example, if Mrs. Smart took two years to repay her indebtedness for the sofa, she might confidently expect the inflation rate to have raised consumer prices by over 20 percent in those two years. The true interest rate is computed by deducting the rate of inflation from the interest rate you actually pay. After all, if inflation gives you far more dollars during the lifetime of your loan, that is a true reduction of your interest payments. So if the inflation rate was 20 percent in those two years, and if Mrs. Smart paid a total of $45 in interest, her true interest rate was less than zero!

The numbers make the point. Mrs. Smart's average balance over the course of the indebtedness was $250. Her average interest cost over the two years was $45 a year. Thus her average interest rate was 10 percent per year on the total purchase price. But because the inflation rate was slightly more than 10 percent per year, Mrs. Smart's true interest cost for buying that sofa was slightly less than zero.

And so it goes. Mrs. Smart

- bought the sofa at a bargain price,
- had the use of it for two years, and
- paid essentially no interest.

In fact, Mrs. Smart's situation was even better than that. In addition to all of the benefits above, Mrs. Smart was able to deduct her interest payments from her income for purposes of computing tax—which lowers her true interest payments far below zero. And if Mrs. Smart's family income was rising as almost everyone's does in the time of inflation, she is able to repay the dollars she borrowed when they were valuable with dollars that became progressively cheaper and more plentiful.

Credit cards are marvelously useful in periods when a MONEYPOWER consumer spots an item that is either reduced in price or is likely to soon be raised in price. With a credit card, the consumer can buy the item immediately, before inflation sweeps the price out of reach. With the pay-back-as-much-as-you-want feature, the consumer can completely control the interest charge. He can let it run if he needs money for something else or if he anticipates receiving many more dollars in the future. Or he can cut off all the interest charges without penalty if he should want to simply by paying off the outstanding balance.

Moreover, inflation, the central economic fact of our era, allows the borrower to borrow at an extremely low true interest rate. What amounts to essentially the same thing, the borrower generally pays with steadily less valuable dollars the debt he acquired in precious dollars.

The credit card user must remember that:

- In our era, buying on credit when a needed item is a bargain is sensible
- The effective interest rate is simply the amount he pays and not any hypothetical rate based on a monthly rate
- Inflation will help him pay off the debt

Credit cards can be veritable lifeboats for intelligent consuming. Even if there were no inflation, it would always be sensible to go into debt to buy items that are good buys (i.e., where the savings greatly exceed the interest cost) unless you have plenty of cash around and will not miss a little of it. In the age of inflation, credit cards and credit borrowing in general make even more sense.

Do the MONEYPOWER rules on borrowing apply to consumer loans and store credit? That depends upon the terms of the store credit. In general, store credit is the revolving variety, similar to credit-card borrowing drill. If the terms are similar to credit-card debt in other ways, the rules are the same.

Beware of so-called Late Charges, which can add greatly to your interest payments. You do not want to incur them and there is no reason to do so. Make certain that they can easily be avoided. If they are not, they can possibly cost so much that they make the entire scheme not worthwhile.

But late charges aside, that credit card you carry around can be a vital weapon in the arsenal of inflation fighting. MONEYPOWER repeats that the hypothetical interest rate should not scare anyone. It has to do with the realm of consumer advocates and cranks. The true interest charge is what you actually pay in dollars and cents, and if you—the consumer—have made a good buy, you will find yourself dollars and cents ahead.

But there are severe limits on just when credit cards can

and should be used. Above all else, no one should use a credit card in the supposition that the bill will never have to be paid. The bill always has to be paid, unfortunately. Shoppers who buy impulsively without needing the items they buy will not be any better off—or just barely—if they pay with a credit card. There is simply no advantage to buying on credit if you buy something you do not need.

Additionally, even if you buy something you need, there is no advantage to buying it with a credit card unless

- its price is lower than it normally is, or
- the price is expected to rise in the future by more than the interest charge, or
- you expect your income to rise by so much more than the interest charge that the true interest charge is zero or close to it.
- you are low on cash and do not want to lay it out—and again need the object now.

Taking these one by one, it is obviously not sensible to buy an item whose price is stable and add on to it the price of interest. In time of financial emergency, we all do it, but it is not sensible.

Similarly, if you expect your income to remain stable over the years—such as in a retirement situation—you cannot expect to repay the valuable dollars you borrowed with plentiful dollars generated by inflation. Thus you are incurring interest charges without acquiring the useful benefits of inflation to help pay off the debt. Do not do it unless you are in an emergency situation.

Credit cards can be of great value in beating inflation if properly used, just as all credit can. But used as a substitute for good sense, they can lead to catastrophe—and have done so. Remember that credit cards are a bridge of money, and the image will help guide you into making sound MONEY-POWER purchasing decisions.

17

Car Leasing: A Shell Game

One of the largest items of expense for any ordinary citizen is his car. We all love our cars, but they cost a great deal of money no matter how they are handled. MONEYPOWER strategy has several ways of lowering the cost of acquiring cars and using them, however. As with all MONEYPOWER strategies, the key is to take advantage of inflation and make it work for you rather than against you. There are forces of inflation at work in the car market just as in all other markets. MONEYPOWER can put you behind them instead of under them.

The hottest trend in today's car market is leasing cars instead of buying them. Millions of people who once plunked down their money and bought their cars outright now lease them from cheerful leasing companies. All of the major car manufacturers' retail outlets have gotten in the leasing business as well.

Supposedly, the appeal of leasing a car instead of buying it is that the lease customer gets special, unspecified tax and business advantages and also does not have to tie up his hard-earned money in car payments. Instead, the customer can use his money to make more money. So the argument runs.

In fact, car leasing—except in special situations—is almost always a contra-inflationary strategy. MONEYPOWER warns that unless you are in special circumstances, which will be described later, you should forget about leasing a car. It makes about as much sense—in the age of inflation—as renting a house instead of buying it.

For the individual—as opposed to the business—most of the much touted mysterious benefits of leasing a car simply do not exist.

If one takes a look at the workings of car leasing step by step one gets a good idea of just how bad a deal it actually is. The customer first goes to a leasing company and tells them what kind of car he wants, with what kind of equipment. If he is a savvy MONEYPOWER customer, he then bargains with the leasing company for the total cost of the car. If he is more relaxed, he simply lets the leasing company fix the price.

Then the leasing company computes the monthly leasing cost based on the total value of the car, whether the lease is for thirty-six or forty-eight months, and whether or not the lease is open ended. Generally, the lease costs less per month the longer the term of the lease.

In an open-end lease, a value is assigned to the car at the end of the lease. If the car is worth less than that value at the end of the lease, you, the customer, have to pay the difference between the actual value and the "value liability." If the car is worth more than your value liability, you may buy the car at the value liability anyway. The leasing companies make an effort to set the value liability so that this does not happen.

At the end of a "closed-end" lease, you need only walk away from your car. There is no further responsibility. A closed-end lease usually costs slightly more than an open-end lease.

Once the monthly payment has been computed, the customer must pay a "capital reduction payment" to insure that the leasing company has something holding you to that car, and to make certain that they have some income from the car immediately. The capital reduction payment is usually no more than 10 percent of the value of the car and often less. Sometimes if a buyer wants to assure himself a substantially lower monthly rental, he can pay a larger capital reduction cost.

Occasionally there is also a security deposit collected on the lease of a car, but this is by no means a uniform proposition. And then the customer takes the car out and starts paying the monthly payments.

It is the exact opposite of what the customer should do. In the era of continuous high inflation, the customer should always use borrowed money to buy an asset that will increase in value. A car does not usually increase in value, but in the age of inflation, it loses its value slowly—sometimes more slowly than the customer pays it off. That makes it a good MONEYPOWER buy.

The leasing customer does not acquire any equity at all in a valuable asset. When he has paid his money, he has gotten the use of the car—which is no mean acquisition—but he has no asset value in the vehicle—unless one counts the option to buy it as a used car.

In stark contrast, the car buyer gets equity and inflation-beating advantages from the word go. The typical car buyer pays about 20 percent down and finances the rest over three or four years. As soon as the car buyer has put down his down payment, he has some equity in the car. Generally, the monthly payments for financing a car are more than the monthly payments for leasing a car—although they will be only slightly more. And, at the end of the payment term, the car buyer has a valuable asset. Note well that used cars are an extremely rapidly rising component of the Consumer Price Index. As soon as you drive that car off the showroom floor, you have a used car. Generally, it will not rise in value—although occasionally it does—but by the time you have finished paying it off, it will be worth a surprisingly large amount.

The lease customer has nothing when he is finished paying except a possible option to *start* buying the car—at the point in time when most buyers would have finished paying for their cars.

Repeat this lesson to yourself: In times of inflation it is good to be a holder of durable goods that have appreciated in value. A car is such a good. A car buyer gets all the advantages of inflation applying to his car. A car lessee gets none of them.

Moreover, the car buyer, especially the car buyer who buys with borrowed money, gets all the advantages of borrowing in the era of continuous inflation.

- He can deduct a very large fraction of his monthly payments on the car because they are interest costs, generating significant tax savings
- He can repay the valuable dollars he borrowed with far more plentiful dollars, as inflation floods him and everyone else with money

The lessee on the other hand has absolutely no tax deductions arising from the leasing process unless he uses the car in a tax-deductible manner for business purposes, in which case he can deduct the fraction of the time he uses the car for business multiplied by the monthly cost of the car multiplied by twelve.

The car buyer can deduct not only the interest costs, but— if he uses the car for a legitimate business purpose—he can also deduct the depreciated value of the car. That is, he can set a legitimate lifetime for the car and depreciate its value over the car's lifetime. This is a matter requiring the attention of an accountant. But generally, the car buyer can get his interest deduction *plus* the depreciation deduction, which will greatly exceed the deduction for monthly leasing of a leased car.

(In general, tax questions are beyond the scope of MONEY-POWER. But when a tax question impinges upon inflationary considerations, it becomes relevant. There is so much misleading conversation around concerning the tax advantages—supposed—of leasing, that here MONEYPOWER had to set the record straight.)

The net of it is that for the ordinary citizen leasing a car simply makes no economic sense at all. There are no MONEY-POWER inflation-beating benefits and no tax benefits. The lease customer is contenting himself with being a passenger in someone else's car, while that someone gets the advantages of owning something that appreciates or depreciates very slowly in the age of inflation.

(And it is interesting to notice—with numbers—just what happens to a used car. After three years a used car in good condition might well be worth 70 percent of what it cost new. That means the customer has gotten three years of use of the car for only 30 percent of its cost, plus the cost of interest on the loan, which is tax deductible. It is certainly true that the 70 percent figure—obtained from National Automobile Dealers' Association blue books—represents nominal dollars, unadjusted for inflation. But even with adjustments, the good used car still retains an enormous amount of its value and provides its owner with a great deal of transportation for a bargain price.

(That high used-car value is the exact analog of the increase in value of used houses. Although car values do not increase, because of inflation their values decrease slowly.)

There are special situations, to be sure, that urge consideration of leasing a car. For example, if a man is starting out in business and needs a prestige car to create a good image, he may be able to lease an elegant car with a rather small down payment. The monthly payment will be tax deductible to the extent that the car is truly used for business. And the car might be considered an earning asset if it generates business. But even in that situation, the man who can buy his car will do better than the man who must lease.

If a person has the opportunity—which few of us have—

to put his money to use at an excellent rate of return, he might as well lease the car and invest his money elsewhere. If he has figured out how to beat the tables at Monte Carlo, for example, his down payment on a car would be far better spent at Monte. But since so few of us can beat the tables at Monte with any consistency, the money might with far more certainty be invested in a car. (In all seriousness, a car is a far safer bet than almost any alternative legal investment.)

And there is a third reason—the most sensible of all—to lease a car. Although there is little economic sense to doing it, leasing a car can make a lot of common sense if the leasing company provides good care for the car. The treatment of car owners by service departments of dealers has become a national disgrace. A person who decides that he will sacrifice the inflation gains of buying a car for the peace-of-mind gains of leasing a car with an excellent service plan cannot be faulted. The waste of human life involved in getting a car fixed by a recalcitrant car dealer is so tragic that anything that reduces it is sensible even if the money cost is substantial. The unfortunate fact is, however, that the normal car lease

- carries with it service through a normal car dealership,
- without any special provisions for better service, and
- with free repairs only during the life of the warranty.

Leasing a car can save trouble also at the end of the lease when the lessee can simply turn in his car without having to sell it as a used car. But for that small bit of peace of mind, the lessee pays richly.

The exact figures will vary enormously depending upon locale, the type of car, the precise nature of the lease, the rate of interest on the car loan, and other factors. But MONEY-POWER research showed that on a 1977 Cadillac Seville, a purchaser with a forty-eight-month, 13 percent loan on 80 percent of the cost came out $7,000 ahead at the end of three years compared to a thirty-six-month closed-end-lease customer. That amounts to almost 50 percent of the cost of the car. It is a sobering calculation.

Whenever the MONEYPOWER consumer is tempted to lease a car, he would do well to think. What does the man who owns the leasing company do with his money? He buys cars, uses them in his business, gets fabulous interest and depreciation deductions, and then winds up with valuable used assets— made even more valuable by runaway inflation. The car-leasing-company owner most definitely does *not* lease his cars for himself. He buys, and so should you.

18

Foreign Cars: A Hedge
on Wheels

One of mankind's undying dreams, somewhat like the dream of the Fountain of Youth or the Philosopher's Stone, is the automobile that would not depreciate in value as it got older. Unfortunately, there is no such thing except for rarely occurring phenomena. But there is a MONEYPOWER way to use inflation to get a car that will make the most money for you in terms of keeping its value. It is an easy way, and almost anyone who needs a new car can do it.

To understand just how it works, the MONEYPOWER investor should cast his mind back to the chapter about speculating in foreign currencies. The reader will remember that in times when the Yankee dollar is losing value through inflation at a faster rate than the German mark and the Japanese yen, the number of dollars required for a given number of yen or marks rises dramatically. Put otherwise, if you happen to have a bundle of yen or marks, you can—during a period of inflation—exchange them for a steadily larger number of dollars.

(With numbers it is clearer. If there are 200 yen to the dollar, 200,000 yen will bring you a round $1,000. If the dollar gets weaker and the yen gets stronger, and if the yen becomes worth 150 to the dollar, your bundle of 200,000 yen will bring you $1,333.33.)

The entire key to the MONEYPOWER way of acquiring a depreciation-resistant car is to have a car that approximates one of those bundles of yen or marks. To put it as clearly as possible, a Japanese or German car is made of steel, cloth, paint, and rubber. But it is also a valuable bundle of yen or marks. It is a hedge against the decline of the dollar—on wheels.

If the MONEYPOWER investor looks at it with numbers, everything becomes clearer. First, remember the postulate of car prices, which runs: Used-car prices follow new-car prices closely. Then imagine a 1974 Honda Civic, which cost $3,500 in the United States at that moment in 1974 when it was purchased. At that time the yen was worth about 294 to the dollar. That means the Honda Civic was worth about 1,029,000 yen.

Now comes 1979. The car has declined in value by about 40 percent, as used cars do over the course of four years. But in the meantime something dramatic has happened to the relation of the dollar to the yen. The dollar has declined to the point where only 210 yen are required for one dollar. Back in Japan, the Honda Company is still cranking out those Hondas. But there has been some inflation in Japan, and the price of the Honda has risen by perhaps 20 percent in yen. Thus that 1978 Honda costs 1,234,800 yen FOB Tokyo.

Translated back into good old U.S. dollars at Honest John's Honda in Anytown, U.S.A., that Honda is going to cost about $5,900. Why has it gone up so much? Because the value of the currency of the country that makes it has gone up by almost 60 percent.

As the new 1978 Honda goes up over $5,900, the used-car price follows it ineluctably. That 1974 Honda has declined by 40 percent, but it has declined by 40 percent not from its price in 1974, *but below the price in 1978.* That 1974 Honda is worth about 60 percent of the value of a new Honda, or about $3,540.

The very same Honda that cost $3,500 in 1974 will sell at retail in 1978 for slightly more than when new. It happens because

- the value of the yen rises dramatically as U.S. inflation outruns Japanese inflation, and
- the value of the new Hondas rises correspondingly, and
- the value of the used Hondas follows the value of new Hondas.

As the forces of inflation have been unleashed to make that 1974 Honda rise in value, it becomes the virtual Fountain of Youth of used cars.

The exact same phenomenon happens to all Japanese cars, not just Hondas. And, as the value of the German mark rises markedly from year to year, the value of new German cars rises drastically—who would ever have imagined a $6,000 Volkswagen beetle?—and this raises the value of used German cars correspondingly.

The MONEYPOWER strategy tells us that buying the cars of countries whose currencies have appreciated along with the rate of inflation—as with yen and marks—is the best general automotive hedge against inflation. The car buyer who puts his money down for a Mercedes or a Subaru is buying not only transportation but a bundle of rapidly appreciating foreign currencies. In a more cautious and circumscribed way, he is speculating in foreign currencies but with almost no downside risk. After all, he still has the four wheels, no matter what happens to the currency.

There are a few real-world constraints on the process, which the MONEYPOWER investor must know before he gets behind the wheel.

First, the rise of foreign—Japanese and German—car prices cannot go on forever. At some point the American consumer is so shocked at the price of these little cars that he simply stops buying them. At that point, the importer must lower his price and the ever-increasing price of Volkswagens stops rising. In the real world, we have apparently not yet reached that point, because well-equipped Hondas are now $9,000. But at some moment in the future, the prices will probably moderate somewhat.

Second, as the price of foreign cars escalates, American manufacturers do just what you would expect them to do. They raise the prices of their cars.

GM, Ford, and Chrysler want money just like everyone else, and so they lift their prices closer to the prices for the corresponding foreign models. This means that owners of American used cars reap a bonanza. Their cars follow the prices of the new cars and rise as well but not as far. This is not a bad thing for the foreign-car owner. It simply means that many people are doing well off the rise in prices of cars from Japan and Germany.

Third, and most important, no car buyer should expect his Datsun or Audi or any other car to go up fast enough so that in real constant dollars—adjusted for inflation—his car retains all of its value. That simply never happens except in the case of models that are suddenly in great demand. Even if a Honda Civic rises in value from a new price of $3,500 in 1974 to a used price of $4,000 in 1978, it has not kept up with inflation. In those four years there has been about 32 percent inflation, while the car has risen in value by about 14 percent. And most car price rises are not even that large.

The MONEYPOWER strategy on car buying will not make you rich. It is not like investing in real estate. It will minimize your real outlay for a car by maximizing its value as a used car. But do not be fooled by prices in unadjusted dollars. No matter how good they seem, they rarely keep up with inflation. The MONEYPOWER strategy will give you the best buy. It will not make you a millionaire.

Once again, it is crucial to emphasize that Hondas and Mercedes are used as examples only. The phenomenon applies to German and Japanese cars generally.

A cautionary note: The rise in the value of foreign currencies relative to the dollar is not monotonic and smooth. There are periods in which the dollar actually gains on the yen and the mark. When the United States is going into a recession while the exporting countries are going into a boom or inflation is just such a time. The trends MONEYPOWER describes are long term. There can be and are short-term countercurrents.

Still, for most families, a car is a significant item of expense. There is absolutely no reason at all to forgo buying it in the most sensible MONEYPOWER way.

Certain dealers will occasionally show the prospective car buyer charts and graphs that purport to prove that their cars retain their value as used cars. And sometimes those proofs are valid. But as a general rule, exceptionally high resale values of domestic cars are based on fads and fashions in car models. While they last, a buyer can do well by following them. But in the long run, betting on inflation is a far surer bet. MONEYPOWER advises the car buyer to lay down his chips on continuing inflation, rather than on a seven-day wonder with denim upholstery.

Many people have lost their shirts betting on a certain look or a certain curve. Few people have lost betting that there will be more inflation.

19

Retirement: Start Early

Sometimes clichés are true. One of the truest is that inflation strikes hardest at those living on fixed incomes, particularly the retired. As a mathematical certainty, inflation will take more of a toll on those who have no opportunity to work harder, change jobs, bargain with their employers, or do any of the many things that the working younger citizens can do to raise their incomes along with inflation. The retirees of America are sitting ducks for every blast of the inflationary cannon, raising their living costs while their defenses—their incomes—remain stuck at a painfully low level.

Retirees are America's fastest-growing major population category. By 1980 there will be at least 28 million persons over sixty-five, of whom three-quarters will be either retired themselves or dependent upon retired spouses. For almost 60 percent of these people, pensions and interest from savings are their sole source of income. That means six out of ten have no inflation-keyed earnings at all to protect them from the inflationary storms.

Social security, which covers almost all retirees to some extent, is adjusted for inflation. At one time in the recent past, it was even rising faster than inflation. But social-security income is for most people so much lower than their preretirement income that even though inflation indexing helps, it does not completely solve their basic problem of too little income.

For example, for a couple living on $300 a week before retirement, their social-security payments might be a maximum of $400 a month, nontaxable, barring some special disability. Even if that social-security payment rises as fast as inflation, the gap between the payment and what the couple needs to maintain their preretirement standard of living will be immense.

More than half of America's retirees have some other income from a second pension or savings interest, but these payments too do not add up to even close to the preretirement earnings.

The stark fact is that the average retiree or retired couple can expect to have an income of slightly less than half their preretirement income—including withdrawals from savings!

Anyone who knows how difficult maintenance of a desirable standard of living is while working can imagine how painful the halving of that income is. And the discomfort is especially acute when the cost of living continues to soar after retirement while the income stays at the same level.

Retirement is a special, extremely serious case for MONEY-POWER care in planning and execution. When age and fatigue reduces the ordinary worker to a state in which he can no longer exchange sweat for bread, he realizes how crucial it is to have his money working for him. And if he has foresight, the MONEYPOWER investor realizes just how crucial acquiring capital is while he is still in his prime and has the chance.

In the American system, even the most ordinary wage slave has the opportunity to acquire some capital, which will take care of him when he grows old. Through the MONEYPOWER techniques set out earlier, the intelligent investor can use the forces of inflation to make more money for himself during bad times than during good times.

The inescapable facts of life are that it is crucial to start work on the acquisition of capital at the earliest possible stages of one's work life. If an investor allows himself to begin to build against the vicissitudes of advanced age at an early

stage—and only if he begins at an early stage—the stringency
of inflation can be avoided at the most difficult moments.

It is simply too late to start thinking about retirement a
year or two before the moment of the gold watch and the
speeches and the rubber chicken. If a worker begins ten years
before retirement to acquire the estate he needs to safeguard
himself and his family, he would have a bare minimum of
time to get the job done. Ideally, and sensibly, a worker will
start acquiring that pool of money he needs while he is still
in his prime working years. If the process begins while the
worker's wages are rising in both real and nominal terms, he
gets into that happiest of circumstances:

- buying valuable, rising assets,
- with scarce borrowed dollars, and
- repaying with plentiful inflated dollars.

The crunch for the farsighted MONEYPOWER investor will
simply never come at all. He buys when buying is painless,
and he has the assets when he desperately needs them.

But when the worker reaches the age of sixty-one or sixty-
two, and he can start crossing off the days until his retirement,
it is simply too late to do anything meaningful about protecting
himself. If the day of retirement comes and all the retiree
has coming in is his social-security check and a small pension—
and most of the pensions are very small—it is simply and
tragically too late to do anything but live frugally and hope
that the day does not come when the cupboard is bare. MONEY-
POWER cannot help a person in that situation, because he
has no money to play with. He or she must use every penny
simply to pay the bills.

MONEYPOWER must turn its attention to the more fortunate
family, whose members have followed a sensible strategy to
defeat inflation and now have some money or some property.
Those people too are faced with critical choices about how
to array their financial assets to ward off inflation and to protect

themselves into the future. And for them, MONEYPOWER is made.

First, a look at the dimensions of the problem. Suppose that the United States continues to suffer from a rate of inflation of 10 percent for the foreseeable future. That means the cost of living doubles every seven years and three months.

Suppose that a farsighted couple have socked away the considerable sum of $250,000 in a savings account paying 5½ percent. Each year that account yields the helpful sum of $13,750. In the first year of the couple's retirement, the interest can buy quite a lot, but look at this table of what the interest is worth in constant dollars (adjusted for inflation) for each year after retirement.

Year	Return in Constant Dollars
1	$13,750
2	$12,375
3	$11,137
4	$10,024
5	$ 9,021
6	$ 8,119
7	$ 7,307
8	$ 6,576
9	$ 5,919
10	$ 5,327
11	$ 4,794
12	$ 4,314
13	$ 3,882
14	$ 3,494
15	$ 3,145

Although the interest rate varies, the principle is always the same.

By the time the retired couple become octogenarians, their

comfortable stake has vanished to almost nil significance. Or, the size of the problem might be imagined by another approach. Suppose that the couple are counting on having a substantial nest egg left for them to dip into when they reach their mid-seventies. Imagine that they start off with $250,000 in cash savings, which is a very substantial amount, and many times more than the average savings of a retired couple. If that money is in the bank at 5½ percent interest, it will double in value in about thirteen years. But if inflation is roaring along at 10 percent, as it has lately, the cost of living will have quadrupled in approximately the same time. The $250,000 of purchasing power the couple owned has shrunk to $125,000 worth, while in the bank at interest! Again the interest rate may vary, but the principle is always the same.

Of course, if the couple put their money into an annuity, the problem is eased for the duration of the annuity. An annuity differs from an interest-bearing savings account in that the annuity guarantees to pay a certain amount per year, but does so by taking something from both capital and interest each year. At the end of the stated period of the annuity, there is nothing left at all—no income, no interest, no savings. And while the income from the annuity might represent a comfortable sum for the life of the annuity, it puts the retirees in the agonizing position of hoping that their personal span of years expires before that of the annuity.

The lesson to be learned is that even a comfortable sum of money becomes uncomfortably small very soon during the period of continuous high inflation. Even prestigious sums yield embarrassing inflation-adjusted returns after a few years. And that lump sum you were planning to leave your grandchildren so that they might carry on missionary work unhindered by sordid money matters dwindles to a paltry stipend in the withering heat of inflation.

Most important of all, the average retiree or retired couple do not have anywhere near $250,000 at the time of retirement.

How then, given the rate of inflation, given the inadequacy of most pensions and income-maintenance programs, given the limited resources available to most retirees, how can the wolf of inflation be kept from the sliding glass doors? Basically, the answer is by

- borrowing cleverly—even in old age;
- judiciously cashing in real-estate equity; and
- carefully investing cash in short-term, high-interest-rate instruments.

Once a couple reaches the age of retirement, they are by definition no longer suited to the MONEYPOWER strategy of acquiring real estate. After all, they cannot repay valuable dollars with plentiful dollars inasmuch as they have stopped working. But, on the other hand, if they have behaved sensibly, they already have at least one dwelling that they own themselves.

About 80 percent of retired couples own their own homes when they retire. About 45 percent of retirees living alone own their own homes. Usually they have owned the homes for a long time and have significant equity in the dwellings. This equity is the centerpiece of the MONEYPOWER strategy for retired people who want to beat inflation.

The exact contours of the MONEYPOWER plan vary according to the circumstances and needs of each retiree. But the basic element is the same: By refinancing their homes, retirees can take a great deal of cash out of their homes without having to sell them and move to unfamiliar hearths. MONEYPOWER tells us the extraordinary fact that inflation is raising the value of homes so rapidly that the retired person need never expect to pay back the proceeds of his refinancing out of his income. Inflation will pay it back without taking money out of the retiree's all-too-limited purse.

This sounds extraordinary, but it is a fact of life in the era of continuous inflation. House prices rise so fast that loans can be paid off either with other loans or with the proceeds of the sale of the house upon the demise of the surviving spouse. Meanwhile, the money the retirees got from refinancing their house is earning interest at a good rate, helping them to live out their declining years in dignity.

Before MONEYPOWER goes into specific cases, a look at the mathematics of the general principle of refinancing and paying off the refinancing with refinancing might make the entire principle clearer.

Suppose that Mr. and Mrs. Older are approaching retirement rapidly. They consult their bankbooks and their pension plan. They find that they will not have as much money as they will need to live adequately, considering the rapid rate of inflation. They have their own house, completely paid off, in Oak Park, Illinois. It is now worth $70,000.

A year before retirement, Mr. Older approaches the Continental Soldier Bank (a fictitious bank) and asks to refinance his house. He gets a loan for 60 percent of the value at the rate of 11 percent. His term is twenty-five years and his monthly payment is $411.65.

The first day after he gets the proceeds of the loan, Mr. Older takes his $42,000 (60 percent of $70,000) and puts it into Treasury bills yielding 9.9 percent. He buys some that are brand new, some that mature in six months, and some that mature in between. He buys so that one-sixth of them will mature every month for the next six months. In other words, he arranges things so that he gets a regular monthly income from the T-bills at a rate of 9.9 percent per year. His yearly yield will be about $4,200, and his monthly take will be $346.

Now anyone can see that Mr. Older will have to pay each month more than he will make from the mortgage. After all, his monthly mortgage payments are $411, and his monthly interest at best is $346. Where then, is the advantage?

The advantage is that Mr. Older can pay off the payments

on the refinancing with part of the proceeds of the refinancing. To simplify the example completely, suppose Mr. Older takes $3,600 of his loan proceeds and puts it in a drawer and uses it to pay off his loan. Each month he will take $300 out of that drawer and add to it $111 of interest on his T-bills, and he will make his mortgage payment.

He still will have another $205 in interest to apply to his living standard. The next year, Mr. Older does the exact same thing. He takes some of the principal amount of the loan, some of the interest, and pays off the year's payments on the loan.

Of course, his capital in T-bills will steadily dwindle as he dips into it for cash to pay his bills.

And also, of course, as Mr. Older's capital dips, the interest he will accrue on his invested capital will also diminish. In this sense, the procedure of taking money out of the house via a second mortgage and then using both interest on the proceeds and the proceeds themselves is similar to an annuity. An annuity uses both interest and principal to pay off a stated sum for a stated number of years, and so does Mr. Older's use of the proceeds of a second mortgage.

But here is a crucial difference between taking the money out of a home and purchasing an annuity. When the term of an annuity is up, that is the end of everything—capital and interest. The exact opposite happens when using the equity in a home. Because of inflation, that equity rises so fast that by the time a homeowner has exhausted both principal and interest, he can refinance his home again, pay off the old loan, and get a new loan just as large.

Look at Mr. Older's situation again to understand with numbers. After about seven years, Mr. Older will have exhausted the proceeds of his first refinancing. But by the end of that seven years, the value of Mr. Older's home will have risen by at least 100 percent, according to recent rates of increase. That means the house will be worth about $140,000.

Mr. Older will owe about $15,000 on his first refinancing at the end of seven years. He can—still using a conservative figure of 60 percent—refinance his home to the tune of $84,000 (60 percent of $140,000.) He uses $15,000 of his $84,000 to pay off the first loan. He can then start the process all over again. He will put the money in notes and use the interest to service the mortgage and to live on.

MONEYPOWER emphasizes that the exercise through which Mr. Older has just gone is not recommended as an actual real-life gesture. It was simply an example to explain a general principle. The general principle is that a home rises so rapidly in value that the homeowner can use the equity in the house and not come close to exhausting the value of the house as a source of income. A house in an inflationary era throws off capital-gains income so fast that the homeowner who can take out the capital gains in the form of refinancing can pay off the loan with the fresh capital-gains income and still have income left over. (This is very much the same as the "reverse mortgage" concept which some banks will soon offer. Retirees can borrow on their home and let the home pay off the debt.)

And the point of it all is that a house is an excellent hedge against retirement for the retiree. It will keep up with and ahead of inflation far faster than any other asset that is readily acquired. While taking out refinancing and then refinancing over and over again involves too much aggravation and risk of short-term problems to be feasible for all but the most steely-nerved, the process tells a lot about the value of a house as an emergency source of funds for a retired couple. A house will grow in value as inflation grows. It will serve as a large piggy bank to be broken into when the need arises.

When retirement income finally becomes inadequate to meet increasingly expensive living costs, then and only then should the piggy bank be shattered. The retiree can either refinance his home and take out the money with a second mortgage, or he can sell it and take all the money in a lump. If the retirees are in need of a large sum, it may be best to sell the house. If a smaller amount is necessary, the house can be used as collateral for a second mortgage or a new loan.

The important point to remember is that the house will continue to grow rapidly in value as time goes by. Of all of the retiree's assets, it will appreciate the fastest in all likelihood. The retiree should make it a rule to hold on to the house until he anticipates a crucial need for the money and sell it only then.

When the retiree does sell, he should buy another piece of property if possible, such as a smaller condo or a smaller house. That way he preserves at least some of his equity in a rapidly rising form. Not only that, but when the retiree owns his own home, he can count on constant payments each month, at least for the mortgage. If he rents, he is all too much at the mercy of his landlord—a position no sensible person of any age wants to be in. (Although when one runs low on money in old age, one will often find rental costs are significantly lower than might have been expected.)

After keeping your house as long as possible, there are simply no ideal options for the retiree. No matter which way the retiree goes he faces the prospect of running out of either funds or life. Unless the retiree owns a business that continues to throw off profits at a rate that rises with inflation, he will find that his income will fall—in terms of real purchasing power—no matter what he invests his funds in.

Yes, for the lucky few who have federal government pensions, monthly payments keep up with inflation and then some. But for the rest of us, inflation will eat away more rather than less, month by month. How then to invest one's funds for retirement?

MONEYPOWER recommends that the two least bad options for investing funds are:

- Treasury bills
- Treasury-bill-pegged C.D.'s at banks and savings and loans

As the reader will remember, Treasury bills are instruments designed to raise money for the government for a six-month period. They are extremely liquid and fluctuate very little in price because of their brief length. They are completely guaranteed. As this is written, they yield about 9.5 percent, which will at least keep up with today's inflation if reinvested and will lose ground rather slowly if used for living.

T-bill C.D.'s are instruments issued by banks and savings and loans. They are intended to keep deposits flowing in when interest rates rise elsewhere. They are usually guaranteed by the federal government—although not always—and they bear interest at the rate prevailing for Treasury bills at the time of sale. While this rate will not make you rich, it will about parallel inflation. As the advertisement says, there is a substantial charge for early withdrawal. But this charge will only bring your interest rate down to passbook level. It is never applied against principal.

Bonds and stocks are far too volatile for the retiree unless he is rich and can stand to lose some money. Besides, very few stocks and bonds pay an adequate dividend or coupon to keep up with inflation.

T-bills and T-bill-pegged C.D.'s, on the other hand, are completely liquid and pay a fine return. And since their return is essentially a function of inflation, they will continue to yield a high return while there is high inflation. They can be rolled over at minimal or zero cost and provide a steady flow of funds at high yields.

Remember, though, that inflation will raise your cost of living remorselessly. Once you reach retirement you must already have enough money to tide you over a doubling or a tripling of the cost of living, or worse. If you reach retirement and you have not provided for yourself, you will be too late. Start working now to make sure that inflation does not turn your golden years into years of nightmare and fear. Only having a lot of money coming in will do it. The time to start is now.

Conclusion: Do It!

The struggle against inflation is both melancholy and exciting. It is first melancholy because it is lonely. By all rights of expectation in a democratic, responsive society, the mass of citizens should engage in the contest together. Through the agency of government, the citizenry might wage war upon inflation until peace and price stability returned. Unfortunately, this world does not work quite that way.

The collective of the citizens in the United States of America is organized in the government in Washington, D.C. And the government in Washington, D.C., is the one and only cause of the inflation. Far from organizing the fight against the inflationary enemy, the government *is* the inflationary enemy. The federal government and the federal government alone generates the huge increases in the national stock of money that cause inflation. Business cannot do it. Labor cannot do it. Only the United States government can create inflation, and it does that very well.

We citizens cannot therefore count upon any help at all from our brethren organized as a group. The government will try to confuse the citizens. It will point the finger at one group or another, or one foreign country or another, or one cartel or another. But that is sheer obfuscation. The blame rests squarely in Washington, D.C., and nowhere else. If the citizen allows the federal government to confuse him and make him believe that someone else is responsible, and, worst of all, that the government is going to help him, the citizen is lost.

The citizen must count upon himself and only himself to beat inflation. There is no one else to do it. His boss will not and cannot do it. His union cannot and will not do it.

Only the individual, resting upon his own strength and initiative, can do it. The government can no more help you beat inflation than aneurysms can help you beat a stroke.

You are the one who will suffer from inflation. You are the one who will benefit from applying the MONEYPOWER strategy. You are the one who has to get it done. You must take the risks. You must energize yourself to work. You must study and think things through with second-level analysis.

The success of the endeavor rests upon digesting several pieces of knowledge and making certain that you act on them as if they were true—because they are.

First and foremost, times have changed. The days of price stability are gone for a while. Prices are probably never going to fall. The nickel Hershey bar has gone the way of the pterodactyl. The good apartment for $200 a month is as extinct as the gooney bird. The days of reasonable prices are simply gone forever. No one can bring them back.

Price stability is gone, at least for quite some time. Do not bother acclimating yourself to prices as they are today. Do not worry about adjusting to what they will be a year from now. They are going up continuously. The alert MONEYPOWER planner knows that the only constant is constantly rising prices (at least for the reasonable future. Inflation will not last forever, but it will last long enough to apply MONEYPOWER rules).

We are in a new world. It is a new order of continuous turmoil and eruption in prices, similar to the eruptive processes that created this world. New landscapes of prices are made and unmade with violent rapidity. The man who will triumph in this new era is the man who realizes that he is in the middle of continual, unending price trauma. He will plan on an ever-rising level of prices, an ever-rising level of income, and a flood of constantly cheapening dollars with which to pay off debts. He will know to look at interest rates with one eye and the rate of inflation with the other so that he judges how high interest rates really are.

He will know that painful as it is, he lives in a time of

uncertainty and flux. And once he adjusts to living in a new
world, with a new atmosphere and new rules, he is ready to
triumph over inflation—through his own understanding of the
inflationary process and *by himself.*

The man who uses inflation to grow rich and live better
will also know that he must take risks. The only courses of
action that are riskless in today's world are those that lead
to financial loss and heartbreak. It is a tragedy that innocent
people cannot live their financial lives in serenity without getting hurt. If the world were as it should be, people could
work and save and come out ahead. In America in our era,
people who work and save are losing money every minute of
every day. Only those who take risks are making money.

The world has become so convoluted and bizarre in fact
that only those who take financial risks avoid the certainty
of financial loss. Borrow for houses. Borrow for gold. Borrow
for foreign currencies. But borrow, risky though it is, and
you will make money. Leave your money in a savings account
and other people will make money off your labor and thrift.

It is time to unlearn the lesson that it is wrong or shameful
to be in debt. There is nothing wrong with it. There is something wrong with losing $5 of every $100 in your savings account every year. There is the real tragedy. The victory is in
making money with borrowed money. The true masters of
their fates do it as a matter of course.

Another painful lesson: Nothing is simple any more. The
man who wants to ride atop the crests of inflation to make
money must study and learn how inflation works—and how
it works for him. The old rules are worthless. The classic
verities of personal finance have been stood on their heads
by long-term inflation. If you allow yourself to be taken in
by them, you will lose money. A lot of it. Do not let it happen.
Learn the new rules and act on them, and remember that
they take some study.

There is nothing bad about taking a few hours or a few

days with a calculator to try to figure out just how inflation can work for you. Mathematics is your friend and not your enemy in this struggle. Make use of it. History and statistics are your allies. Make the most of them in your campaign.

Daring to risk your money without troubling to risk some of your time to study and learn is insanity. No one has enough money to be so foolish. Study without the spirit of risk is sterile and unproductive sitting. Study and risk taking are the engine and the fuel that will propel you to success in MONEY-POWER.

And one more thing. All inflations eventually come to an end. Even the Weimar inflation of 1923 came to an abrupt halt, leaving some speculators high and dry. The hysterical South American inflations of the 1950s and 1960s have waxed and waned. So it will be here. The present level of inflation may well pale before future levels, but eventually there will be price stability—at least for a time. At some point, the social demand for it becomes so intense that the politicians can no longer ignore it. That may not happen for a decade, but it will happen someday.

It will not come suddenly. Overnight wage and price controls cannot stop inflation dead—at least not for long. Just as pressing on one point of a balloon does not make the balloon stay flaccid, so price and wage controls will not hold down inflation while hot air in the form of money is pumped in. So the MONEY-POWER investor should observe that when wage-price controls come along, some things will not be controlled—land, commodities, precious metals, black-market items—and these things will rise fabulously in price, absorbing all the inflationary energy of the economy.

Gradually, the prices of the uncontrolled items will become so high that the entire economy will go into convulsions. Then the wage-price controls will come off, and the inflation will roar on. Part of MONEYPOWER wisdom is to keep your eye on the uncontrolled sector and get some of it for your very own. But far more to the point is to realize that wage-price controls are a substitute for fighting inflation. They do not actually fight inflation themselves.

Someday, however, a President will come along who will put the screws on the economy. He will risk unpopularity because of rising unemployment. He will suffer the housing industry to go into the doldrums. And he will cut the federal budget ruthlessly. And if the country goes into recession, he will know that it will not go into a depression because the banks cannot fail. And with that confidence, he will continue to squeeze the inflation out of the economy until it is almost all gone.

There is no sign that such a President is on the scene or in the wings. But eventually, the people will demand that a President stop inflation, and eventually a President will do it. There will be plenty of warning. And prices will not fall. But little by little, they will rise less rapidly. Wages will also rise less rapidly, and shoppers will notice that prices are not changing as fast. Unions and welfare groups will scream. So will some congressmen. And, lo and behold, the rate of inflation will come down to tolerable levels.

As earlier chapters have said, that will be the time to liquidate real estate, liquidate gold, liquidate foreign currencies. Trim borrowings and look for high-paying savings instruments. The MONEYPOWER rules will be suspended for a time.

But for now, MONEYPOWER is your map. Now get there.

Index

AAA bonds, 113, 114, 120
aged:
    tax shelters for, 24–25, 26
    see also retirement
American Stock Exchange, 88
American Stock Exchange Index,
    110–111
annuities, 185, 188
apartment houses, rent control and,
    48–49, 147
appreciated property, farms as, 65–
    66
Arabs, farmland purchases of, 64
arbitrage, 31, 50–59
    in currency, see speculation, in for-
        eign currency
    defined, 50
asked price, defined, 80
Aubusson rugs, 127
auctions, 126, 128, 135
Austrian hundred-crown pieces, 79

banks, 35, 48, 54–55, 58, 118–119,
    190–191
    exotic cars and, 130
    in farm financing, 65
    Guaranteed Student Loan pro-
        gram and, 140–141
    lines of credits offered by, 143–144
    services of, 149–150
    see also loans; mortgages; savings

Barnum, P. T., 124
Belgium, diamond cutters in, 132
bid price, defined, 80
bonds, 2, 23–24, 47, 113–116, 147–
    149, 191
    AAA, 113, 114, 120
    corporate, 115
    interest-rate futures and, 147–148
    municipal, 115–116
bond yields, 113–115
borrowing, see loans; mortgages
British pounds, 93, 95, 99
brokerage firms, 150
building codes, 15, 56

California:
    lines of credit in, 143
    mortgage ceilings in, 37, 44
Canada, gold-mining companies in,
    88
Canadian dollars, 99
capital assets, taxes on, 23–24
capital gains, 43, 45, 47, 189
    of farmers, 65, 66
capital-gains tax, 24, 65
car leasing, 169–175
    capital reduction payments in,
        170–171
    in image creation, 173
    occasions for, 173–174
    security deposit in, 171